"*Stephen Adams has written a book that could be a lifesaver for thousands and an encouragement for millions. In a time when six months means 3 million lost jobs, a book on how to 'treat unemployment as a job,' is beyond timely, it is crucial. . . . Many times over the past year I have sat down with a friend who has lost his or her job, and those who had adopted the right attitude were much farther along in their job search or career change. The key tools to finding not just a new job but the right job are all here in* **Back to Work!**, *and written by a man who has lived through two such transitions and who writes from experience and from faith.*"

—HUGH HEWITT
Nationally syndicated talk show host and
New York Times bestselling author

BACK TO WORK!

Create NEW OPPORTUNITIES in the Wake of Job Loss

STEPHEN P. ADAMS

MOODY PUBLISHERS

CHICAGO

Editor: Elizabeth Cody Newenhuyse
Interior Design: Ragont Design
Cover Design: John Hamilton Design
Cover Images: iStockPhoto

ISBN: 978-0-8024-4261-1

We hope you enjoy this book from Moody Publishers. Our goal is to provide high-quality, thought-provoking books and products that connect truth to your real needs and challenges. For more information on other books and products written and produced from a biblical perspective, go to www.moodypublishers.com or write to:

Moody Publishers
820 N. LaSalle Boulevard
Chicago, IL 60610

1 3 5 7 9 10 8 6 4 2

Printed in the United States of America

To my wife, Mary Jane

CONTENTS

PREFACE

So much has changed since *Reinventing Your Career* was originally published in 1996. New wars. New presidents. New technologies. New scandals. New prosperity. And yet, how much is still the same. The economic down-cycle of the early 1990s gave rise to trends like corporate downsizing, outsourcing, reengineering, and repurposing that returned with a vengeance in the Great Recession that began in December 2007. All of which translate into much the same thing: Massive layoffs. Dislocated workers. Home foreclosures. Personal bankruptcies. Fractured families.

I have experienced two more job losses since *Reinventing Your Career* was published. At that time I was taking my first shot at self-employment and had a good run at it for two years under the banner Adams Business Communications: Ideas in Print, Words on Paper. In fact, the public relations firm that had let me go hired me back as an independent contractor when it landed a job that required extra hands. That helped set my market rate (the billable hour formula we discuss in the appendix). Even though this work lasted less than two years, it was a tremendous learning experience that would not be wasted.

Meanwhile, another door opened in Colorado, where I was hired as editor of a denominational magazine, which would involve a great deal of world travel and reporting from the mission field. It seemed like my dream job, the thing I would do until retirement.

How wrong I was. The president of the organization, who had hired me, dropped dead of a heart attack one day on the tennis court. For me, it was the beginning of the end. New vice presidents for my division came and went, and one day my immediate supervisor was forced into retirement. Quickly I went from a valued manager who received excellent performance reviews and annual raises to an employee who could do no right. And then I was asked to leave. This broke my heart. In the midst of the pain, I was diagnosed as clinically depressed and received professional help. Job loss No. 2.

I struggled for years to make a living as a freelance writer and editor for some of the Christian and nonprofit organizations in Colorado Springs under the name Insight Communications. Then an opportunity arose at one of the largest employers in town, a Christian ministry. Its public policy magazine needed an associate editor, and I was back in full-time employment again, doing something that seemed ideal for me. But now I was older, and I found myself feeling like an outsider. When the organization fell on hard financial times, like the rest of America in late 2008, it was no huge surprise when I found myself among the couple hundred who received pink slips. It was called a layoff, but there would be no callbacks. The positions were eliminated, permanently. Job loss No. 3.

This time, so close to retirement age, there would be no starting over. The die is cast. Months of unemployment suggest to me that Loss No. 3 could be the last one because there may be no replacement job. I have to face the possibility that I will either make it in self-employment or I won't.

One other thing that has changed is the title of this book.

Back to Work! is meant as an exhortation to move on, let go of the past, and treat unemployment as a job in itself—not to get frozen in self-pity, discouragement, or rejection. It is an updated version of *Reinventing Your Career* for the 21st century, as major economic disruption is once again upon us like a massive case of déjà vu.

This time, there would be no starting over.

Now, let's pick up where we left off in 1996.

A sign on the wall at the Cuyahoga County Reemployment Services Center in Cleveland, Ohio, may not have been the most appetizing message for a lunchroom, but it got to the point:

"If you have to swallow a toad, don't spend too much time looking at it."

To the jobless people who passed through these halls, the message connected. Losing a job can be like staring eyeball to eyeball with a fat, ugly toad and waiting to see who blinks first. You have two basic choices—let yourself become paralyzed by the unpalatable circumstances or swallow hard and move on.

Often there's a crushing load of discouragement, rejection, self-pity, even shame. Sometimes there's anger and bitterness toward the heartless former employer or a former boss who ought to be wearing a black hat—over his horns. The temptation is to dwell on the past to the exclusion of the future. Counselors encourage the jobless to deal with their circumstances just like a death in the family—allow time for the natural grieving process, then get on with life.

Back to Work! as the name suggests, is about dealing. It's about getting on with life.

What do you do after the pink slip arrives, when your services are no longer needed or your job no longer exists? Blame and resentment won't pay the rent. Unemployment compensation will only keep food on the table for so long. There comes a point where we have to pick ourselves up and, as the Old Blue Eyes song goes, get back into the race. It may be a rat race, but you don't have to be trapped like one. There is healing, and there are ways to prepare to face a future that only promises to present more of the same.

So, that's easy for me to say? Not really. I've been there.

Of life's stressors—traumatic setbacks, disasters, and catastrophes—most people would list events like the death of a child, death of a spouse, and loss of a job. Within a relatively short period of time, I experienced two of those three.

In the late 1980s I was assistant city editor for a newspaper that was experiencing major upheavals in management. In the process I received a pay cut and was assigned to a night shift in a dead-end position—the "bonepile," one coworker called it. But the worst part was family life. It ceased to exist. Every day, my children would come home from school about a half hour after I'd left for work. Every night I would come home to a darkened house where dinner had been eaten, bedtime stories read, and prayers said without Dad.

For nearly two years I struggled with anger and bitterness while I searched fruitlessly for another newspaper job, hating every morning that the sun rose on another day of frustration. In fact, I never did find another newspaper job. My escape then was through a career change. I took a job in public relations, which actually came with a pay increase. But it meant turning my back on a twenty-year newspaper career.

Six years later, I got a lesson in economic reality when two of us at this company were called in on a Monday morning and told our services were no longer needed. I was shocked and shattered. This had never happened to me before. But I was also oddly relieved, having worked under extremely stressful conditions for some time. I didn't know then that relief is the second stage in the grief process, right after the initial shock.

Just fifteen months earlier, my wife and I had lost a child—

a newborn son, who lived two weeks and then succumbed to complications of Rh disease. We had known the circumstances were difficult, but until the last day, we struggled to believe that we were going to take that child home. We were wrong.

In retrospect, I can believe that my work performance over those subsequent months may have been less than stellar due to my sheer emotional exhaustion. I may have inadvertently nominated myself to be one of the employees to walk the corporate plank.

I can also say, however, that some of these experiences were blessings in disguise for the fruit they produced in my life. First, I had to deal with those areas of anger and bitterness in my heart. It became clear that my priorities needed adjusting so that my career was not such a huge idol in my life. Meanwhile, I used those lonely wee hours in a dark house when I came home from work as an opportunity to write fiction, which eventually turned into my first book, *October Holiday.*

In the pages of *Back to Work!* we will meet a few other individuals for whom losing a job was not the end of the world but actually the beginning of a new, if not better, life.

In the first three chapters we will look at the economic and employment upheaval, and then at real case studies of a few individuals whose lives were changed forever. Chapter 4 looks at the downside of staying in a bad job. In chapters 5 and 6 we explore the value of discovering a sense of personal purpose and mission in work life and identifying our strengths. We then meet in chapters 7 and 8 the composite character Jerry Davenport, who takes us through the career counseling process, dealing with emotional and self-esteem issues and then practical job-search skills and strategies. Chapter 9 is a forward-looking examination of new work/lifestyles, such as telecommuting, self-employment, home-based businesses, and the virtual office. Finally, we consider the ultimate mission—our life purpose—in chapter 10.

One way or another, most people have been affected by layoffs and downsizing or know somebody who has. And, as we'll see, everyone is affected, not just those who have lost a job. Those who keep their jobs are indirectly involved through something called "layoff survivor syndrome."

I am reminded of the words of a U.S. president and the angel of the Lord. Franklin D. Roosevelt said in the midst of America's worst depression that the only thing to fear was fear itself. Or, as the angel of the Lord said more simply, "Fear not."

For me, the first battle was casting out anger and fear. (They're really the flip side of each other.) After that, everything else began to fall into place. And, oh yes, one more fruit was produced out of the suffering process:

You're holding it in your hands. Fear not.

1

THE JOB
SQUEEZE

Layoffs. Restructuring. Reengineering. Buyouts.
Downsizing. Rightsizing. Reduction in force. It all
adds up to the same thing: disappearing jobs. An
employment black hole across America.

In 1996, *The New York Times* was telling us just
how bad things were: "On the battlefields of business,
millions of casualties."[1] The big story was a half-
million Americans a year being laid off—some
permanently—with ripple effects for millions of
families.

Fast-forward to 2009, when more than a half-
million Americans *a month* were being laid off early
in the year, and the story was the *Times*, where
economic reality finally reached this far. A hundred
employees were let go, and the remaining workers
experienced a 5 percent pay cut.[2] In February alone,
about 1,500 newspaper journalists were looking for
another situation.[3]

Even though, as of this writing in late summer 2009, the Great Recession of 2008–2009 appears to be easing, or at least "less bad," the same cannot be said about the overall shape of the labor market. According to some forecasts, the U.S. unemployment rate won't return to "normal" levels until 2014. In July 2009, 14.5 million Americans were out of work.[4] Manufacturing and construction have been particularly hard-hit, but so have other white-collar sectors.

So if you're out of a job—you're in good company.

Theories abound on why the current unemployment situation is so dire, even as other indicators, like the stock market, seem to be trending upward. When the financial markets cratered in 2008 and many investors saw serious erosion in their portfolios, consumers stopped spending. The credit crunch affected countless businesses. Large bellwether industries like the automotive Big Three slashed their workforces, in particular GM as the government stepped in to stabilize the company's shaky finances. The housing crash impacted a host of industries from construction to real estate sales to big-box stores.

Moreover, some jobs may be gone forever.

Mortimer Zuckerman, chairman and editor-in-chief of *U.S. News & World Report*, wrote that this was the first recession since the Great Depression to entirely "wipe out all job growth from the previous expansion."[5] Add in some other real-life situations— those who have stopped looking for work or have taken part-time jobs, for example—and the real number would be more like 16.5 percent or 25 million people involuntarily idle, he said. But what about when the economy turns around? Zuckerman again:

> The likelihood is that when economic activity picks up, employers will first choose to increase hours for existing workers and bring part-time workers back to full time. Many unemployed workers looking for jobs once the recovery begins will discover that jobs as good as the ones

they lost are almost impossible to find because many layoffs have been permanent.[6]

Just prior to this major recession, female representation in the workforce was pegged at 49.1 percent, according to Labor Department figures. So, after millions of new job losses, has that number changed? Considering that as high as 80 percent of those pink slips went to males, America is entering the era of the majority-female workforce.[7] Various reasons are given for that disproportionate impact, which tend to boil down to higher-paid individuals being more vulnerable to layoffs but also to the fact that education and health care have been less affected and women comprise the bulk of the workforce in those sectors. But the more serious question may be the long-term impact on a society in which the new norm is the stay-at-home dad.

Family policy expert and political consultant Jim Pfaff offers this perspective on the current situation:

WELCOME TO "POST-POST-INDUSTRIAL AMERICA"

This current recession is unlike anything we have seen in three generations. The surreal landscape on the back end of the "collapse" of financial institutions has distorted the way we have traditionally evaluated the job market. Post-Industrial America is quickly becoming Post-Post-Industrial America, where job seekers find the employment landscape in disarray.

In past recessions America had a strong manufacturing base. Companies like General Motors, Chrysler, Ford, and even American Motors were mainstays even for workers displaced by layoffs who just returned when things got better. Westinghouse, General Electric, Amana, Maytag, and other electrical and appliance manufacturers went though similar cycles of hiring, laying off, and rehiring. Beginning with the dot-com boom in the 1990s, graduating college students found new avenues of opportunity, and the country emerged as a post-industrial economy where intellectual capital had become as valuable as the latest production technology.

The world of finance exploded, too, with abundant venture capital, mergers and acquisitions, and personal investment capital flowing into an ever-expanding investment market. Wall Street was roaring just like many new dot-com start-ups, offering real opportunity for significant long-term advancement for new university grads.

Then, when the Internet boom went bust, it seemed that all the promise of the boom had been short-lived. But it wasn't. Internet companies reformed and retooled. We learned that the Internet was the business platform of the future, and this was the first shakeout of weak players. Dot-commers either rode out the storm or joined forces to build new online companies and services, building upon the lessons learned. Wall Street was banged up and knocked down, too, but quickly returned for another round with little employee displacement. Once again, a recession didn't seem so bad because everyone just hung on until they could jump back on the same merry-go-round.

The recession that began in December 2007, however, is a totally different animal. This time around, many of the newly unemployed will have no choice but to find a new career. This may mean some will have to go backward in their career to find the way back.

THE FUTURE OF JOBS

Only a generation or two ago, it was common for workers to have one career and not unusual even to have the same job all their working days. Lifetime employment was the norm. In 1996 experts were saying the average person would have about ten jobs in a lifetime and three career changes—and in the future would have six to ten career changes in their lives. By May 2009, Sony's "Did You Know" YouTube clip was winding its way around the e-world with a mind-blowing collection of exponential social and technological trends, including this update on the above figures: "The U.S. Department of Labor estimates that today's learner will have 10-14 jobs . . . *by the age of 28*" (Italics added). Other factoids: "1 in 4 workers has been with their current employer for less than a year" and "1 in 2 has been there less than 5 years."[8]

> **The packaging of work in the form of jobs is a mere two hundred years old—and a pendulum swing may be in full reverse.**

Yet, in the scheme of things, jobs are a relatively recent phenomenon. Work itself is as old as the first patch of weeds in the garden after the fall. William Bridges, author of *JobShift: How to Prosper in a World without Jobs*, calls jobs a "social artifact" of the industrial era.[9] Unfortunately, those of us who depend on this social artifact for many of our needs are living in what's been called the Post-Industrial Era:

> The job concept emerged early in the nineteenth century to package the work that needed doing in the growing factories and bureaucracies of the industrializing nations. Before people had jobs, they worked just as hard but on shifting clusters of tasks, in a variety of locations, on a schedule set by the sun, the weather, and the needs of the day. The modern job was a startling new idea—to many people, an unpleasant and even socially dangerous one.[10]

The Industrial Revolution began powering up in England and western Europe shortly after the American Revolution in the late eighteenth century, driven by such breakthroughs as steam-powered spinning machines and looms. Until then, the workplace had been the village, the field, and the home, where farmers, craftsmen, and families did their work without time clocks, employment contracts, and management consultants. Now the factory with its regimentation began to become the norm.

By the early twentieth century, another principle came to the fore—narrow functional specialization and scientific management, as defined by Frederick Taylor, the father of management gurus. This involved breaking jobs down into a large number of simple tasks the worker would repeat over and over with machine-like efficiency under a command-and-control type of supervision. Ironically, today's management consultants counsel quite different approaches—self-directed work teams, participative management, etc. Different times call for different prescriptions.

By 1914, Henry Ford introduced the assembly line, dividing tasks into narrow functional specialties and ushering in the era of mass production. It was the ideal means of manufacturing goods in great quantity with a large population of low-skilled and uneducated workers, many of them immigrants. Companies could train an individual to perform the same job routine repeatedly without requiring a great deal of independent thought. That was left to the growing cadre of supervisory and support personnel.

Under this approach, the United States became the manufacturing giant of the world—the largest producer and exporter of goods with the largest labor force and the highest wages. This remarkable success gave America the highest standard of living in the world, but the U.S. occupation of the catbird seat was far from permanent. The golden era of dominance, according to historians and economists, lasted approximately thirty years, from the end of World War II to the onset of the global economy and the Technology Revolution—1945 to 1975.

The illusion of permanent prosperity coincided with the advent of the baby boomer generation—76 million babies born from 1946 to 1964. The 1960s, though overshadowed by the threat of nuclear war, began with the glow of a Camelot presidency and the belief that America could "bear any burden, pay any price," in the words of John F. Kennedy. Expectations couldn't have been higher. Until her military might became bogged down in Vietnam, it seemed there was little that was not within America's grasp. President Kennedy vowed that America would put a man on the moon before the end of the decade. And, though Kennedy did not live to see it himself, the promise was fulfilled in 1969, when Neil Armstrong took a giant leap for mankind.

Economically, too, America was a juggernaut. But success begat complacency, and without serious competition from abroad—at first—there was little incentive for U.S. manufacturers to worry about down-the-road problems with cost and quality. It became the age of inflation, as workers and companies pursued an upward spiral that eluded President Nixon's wage and price controls. But around the corner lurked two other major forces—consumerism and the quality movement.

Ralph Nader's career as a consumer advocate and corporation basher was launched with the publishing in 1965 of *Unsafe at Any Speed*, an indictment of U.S. automakers for shoddy design and workmanship, as evidenced by General Motors' Corvair. Unwittingly, American manufacturers were setting themselves up as juicy targets once the Japanese and others figured out that they could beat the Yanks at their own game and capture a major portion of the global market with lower-cost, higher-quality goods.

Experts say the wake-up call began in 1973 with the Arab oil embargo, which decisively demonstrated that no nation—not even the U.S.A.—can go it alone and that the price of industrial might is energy dependence. The so-called global economy began to take center stage with the fall of Communism and the unification of Europe under the European Union. Then the Western Hemisphere followed suit with the removal of trade barriers through the North American Free Trade Agreement (NAFTA), whose opponents argued bitterly that it would cost U.S. jobs.

Foreign competition was one of four factors cited by the *New*

York Times in a series published during the recession of the early to mid-nineties. The other three: technological progress that lets machines replace hands and minds, the ease of contracting out work, and payroll cuts to make companies more attractive on Wall Street. To these could be added a generation of baby boomer managers much more willing than the previous generation to trim staff size, and changes in the accounting practices mandated by law. And these factors–among others—are still in play in the current downturn.

THE TECHNOLOGY REVOLUTION

The Technology Revolution began a sharp spike in 1976 with the appearance of the personal computer, which offered the promise of putting mainframe power into the hands of ordinary people. Over the next twenty years, the PC began to redefine the workplace, changing the speed of work and the way literally thousands of different kinds of tasks are carried out. By the 1980s, power was doubling and the price was being cut in half approximately every eighteen months, a phenomenon that became known as Moore's Law. By the 1990s, automakers were pointing out that the brains of their cars were bigger than the computers aboard the Apollo spacecraft.

The greater wonder may be why it's taken so long for this revolution to begin chopping heads.

But this new technology also was beginning to do something else a little less user-friendly: The long-feared specter of automation finally was taking its toll on jobs through industrial robots, computerized machinery, and microelectronic techniques. Soon, even white-collar workers, who had been immune to such vicissitudes in the past, began to fall prey to the pink slip as even those jobs began to disappear.

As long as computers have been around, the greater wonder

may be why it's taken so long for this revolution to begin chopping heads. The answer may involve the ways technology is handled or, especially in the early stages, mishandled. Experts have noted that when the electric motor was first introduced, it took a remarkably long time to change things and fulfill its potential of portable power. At first, it was used simply as a direct replacement for the giant, smoky steam engine that had no place on the factory floor. Its power was transmitted instead to individual machines and work stations through a Rube Goldberg series of belts and pulleys connected to one central driveshaft from the outside.

Eventually, the industrial engineers figured out that there was a more efficient way of doing things, and the next technological corner was turned. Similarly, it wasn't until recent years that the power of computing reached critical mass in the workplace in a very direct human sense. Harry S. Dent Jr., author of *JobShock*, said the tendency at first was to use information technology merely to enhance the old ways of the "paper-shuffling bureaucracy" rather than advance real innovation. Hence the older-generation manager whose desktop computer was little more than a high-tech paperweight. But that's all changing with a vengeance, Dent suggested in a section of his book entitled "Computers Are the New Office Workers."

"Sure, we've had computers in offices," he wrote, "but we haven't used them to real advantage in most organizations. The workplace has been filled with an older generation used to working in a hierarchical command and control system. This generation is less willing to take risks than the newer generation moving into positions of power now and in the future: baby boomers. The members of this newer generation have already proved they will take necessary, calculated risks to bring in new, creative ways of conducting business when they have come into power."[11]

And now, of course, many of the jobless are themselves boomers who wonder if they have a place in today's—and tomorrow's—workplaces.

John Naisbitt and Patricia Aburdene, authors of *Megatrends*, accurately forecast the current situation in their book *Re-inventing the Corporation*, when they predicted a major flattening of the ranks of middle managers in America. Staff managers who supervise people would give way to small groups, work teams, and other self-management structures, according to Naisbitt and Aburdene, and line managers in charge of systems would be replaced by computers.

Their words, published in 1985, seem eerily prophetic now:

> Today, computers are replacing middle managers at a much greater rate than robots are replacing assembly line workers. Once indispensable to senior executives, many middle managers are now watching computers do their job in a fraction of the time and at a percentage of the cost. The whittling away of middle management presents serious problems for all those baby boomers about to enter middle management. The number of men and women between thirty-five and forty-six, the prime age range for entering middle management, will increase 42 percent between 1985 and 1995. Clearly, millions of baby boomers who aimed for middle management will never reach their goal. There simply will not be enough middle management jobs. It is a scary thought for some people.[12]

And that's pretty much what's happened. Various sources agree: The tables have been turned. The majority of laid-off workers now are college-educated, salaried employees who held white-collar jobs. It's a fact that helps account for the way the layoff/firing phenomenon is getting more national attention and publicity.

Something else that's changed big-time is the old adage "Last hired first fired." This relic of the paternalistic corporation when seniority was highly valued began to fall by the wayside in the major restructuring of American business practices during the 1990s. But its real impact was not felt until the major recession of 2008–09, when many thousands of older workers found themselves on the street, some of them for the very first time. What many people were experiencing anecdotally—an apparent disproportionate graying of the unemployment ranks—has been confirmed by the U.S. Equal Employment Opportunities Commission, which reported a 30 percent jump in age-discrimination complaints. As a side effect of the recession, the American workforce faces "an equal opportunity plague" of age discrimination, the EEOC said.[13]

The reasons are varied, including a decline in labor unionism, which used to fight aggressively to enforce seniority rights. Also, recent federal court rulings have been blamed for making age discrimination cases harder to prosecute. (Basically, any other business factor the employer is able to cite for termination automatically nullifies the age factor.) That's why employers are able to get away with jaw-dropping remarks about older workers as "grandpa" or having poor "job fit in this Internet age" or being "pale, male, and stale." But the biggest factor may be the simple correlation between age and pay—i.e., older, more senior employees make more money and cost more to retain. In lean times a company looking to reduce its bottom line can get there faster by casting this group overboard. And for much the same reason males are also over-represented in the jobless pool. "Older white males hurt more by this recession," said a *USA Today* headline over a report on how the problem was hurting "aging Baby Boomers" the worst. And in many ways the blow is more devastating to this group:

> Those above 55 also are spending more time than ever between jobs. Older workers spend an average 27 weeks between jobs, about five weeks longer than younger workers. . . . The loss of a job for an older worker can erase the dominant income of a middle-class family, wipe out savings as retirement nears and deny aging people health insurance when it's needed most.[14]

A NEW SOCIAL CONTRACT

A trend that took off in the recession of the early 1990s has only accelerated during the current downturn: a realization that we, employees, can no longer be dependent on "them," the employers. Even the "best companies to work for" have been quick to cut hours, cut salary, cut staff. The displacements have reached beyond the typically cutthroat Fortune 500 world to such seemingly safe environments as Christian organizations, some of which have laid off scores of employees, including some who had served for decades.

Cliff Hakim, an executive career consultant, wrote in *We Are All Self-Employed* that a new social contract has replaced the old employment paradigm. "Dependence on the organization is obsolete. The familiar employee-employer contract has now been broken. Loyalty to the organization no longer guarantees job security. Workplaces en masse are reshaping themselves to survive and compete, and millions of individuals have lost their jobs."[15]

Companies recognize this on one level but not on another, and so exhibit an institutional split personality, unintentionally sending mixed signals to their workforce. On one hand, they are still exercising old strategies that management consultant David Noer calls "person capturing"—offering benefit plans, recreation programs, group travel benefits, day care, tuition reimbursement plans, comprehensive career planning, raises and promotions by seniority and tenure—originally designed to tie the person to the organization and to be prepared for a predictable future.[16] On the other hand, the new reality is that organizations are really in the process of untying employees in the face of an unpredictable future. Their formal culture, i.e., what they profess, is not in sync with their own operational culture, i.e., what they actually do. In fact, it is even contradictory.

Reality has not entirely caught up with actual practice. Between the idea and the reality, wrote poet T. S. Eliot, falls the shadow. In these times we are living in the shadowlands.

NO TURNING BACK

But when we emerge from the shadowlands, the employees who acknowledge the new reality will be well ahead toward coping with it and even thriving. Having a traditional job, a regular paycheck, and fringe benefits can breed a kind of security-mindedness that crushes the spirit and rots the bones when it's withheld. For generations, Americans have assumed that such security is our birthright, and we do not handle it well when that security is withdrawn. It's the glass-is-half-empty attitude instead of "God's grace shed on thee" when compared with the standard of living almost anywhere else in the world.

Judith M. Bardwick, a management consultant and psychologist, says entitlement results when people "don't have to earn what they get" and soon "take for granted what they receive." In *Danger in the Comfort Zone*, she said the entitlement disease is not just a rap against lower-level workers. It's also hard at work among high-level corporate executives of large organizations that "freeze wages, lay workers off, and give executives big raises."[17]

Paradoxically, this "danger in the comfort zone," according to Bardwick, is at its greatest when "life is too safe." Considering the current turmoil and upheaval, could that mean America is actually becoming healthier? Could it be that Americans need to recover some of the self-reliance and God-reliance that made the United States great? "By protecting people from risk, we destroy their self-esteem," Bardwick wrote. "We rob them of the opportunity to become strong, competent people. Facing risk is the only way we gain confidence, because confidence is the result of mastering challenge. Confidence is an internal state. It cannot be given; it can only be earned. The only way to get genuinely confident is to be familiar with fear and then conquer it."[18]

Perhaps all of us as believers need to reread Paul's advice in 2 Thessalonians 3: "For you yourselves know how you ought to imitate us, because we were not idle when we were with you, nor did we eat anyone's bread without paying for it, but with toil and labor we worked night and day, that we might not be a burden to any of you" (vv. 7–8 ESV).

David Noer gives similar advice in a discussion of what he calls layoff survivor sickness, his description of the effects on organizations of contemporary downsizing. In *Healing the Wounds*, Noer says that workers who survive the ax become demotivated, feeling "a deep sense of violation." And their organizations often fail to reap the touted benefits for all that pain.

> Organizations that once saw people as assets to be nurtured and developed began to view those same people as costs to be cut. . . . Organizations institute layoffs to cut costs and promote competitiveness but afterward often find themselves worse off than before. All they have gained is a depressed, anxious, and angry workforce. At the very time they need spirit and creativity, they enter into global competition with a risk-averse team.[19]

Noer says a major part of the survivor sickness is denial—going on with business as usual as if nothing has changed when, in fact, things are never going to be the same. Workers must approach employment with a less dependent and more autonomous, entrepreneurial attitude in the future, especially in assessing their own self-worth, Noer says. "Don't place your spiritual currency in the organizational vault," he writes.[20]

Rather—and we will pursue this more extensively later in this book—this may be the time to look at life from a more adventuresome perspective, not leaning on our "own understanding" but in everything we do acknowledging the God who will make straight our paths (Proverbs 3:5–6 ESV).

In these turbulent times numerous businesses have had to make radical changes to survive. They have had to reinvent themselves. And individuals may have to do much the same thing—reinvent their careers, and, in so doing, learn the truth of Psalm

37 and a Father who wants to give us the desires of our hearts.

It's time to meet a few people who have had to rise to the occasion.

2

DISPOSABLE
PEOPLE

There's no getting around it: Being let go hurts.

A job loss may not have been meant personally,
but it's tough not to take it that way. It cuts to the
very heart of who we are and threatens to overwrite
our identity with death language: Rejected. Inferior.
Failure. No good. Second-rate. Loser. In the midst
of the circumstances and the pain, how easy it is
even for believers to forget the Maker's original
imago dei imprint upon us—the seal that says "in
His image." That pink slip and the dehumanizing
way in which it is too often delivered are far more
real and tangible in the moment.

"MY LAYOFF WAS A SPEAR
AIMED AT MY IDENTITY"

Three months before the ax fell, Steve Kipp, a twenty-one-year employee of a large Christian ministry, had a dream that it was coming—and this time his neck would be on the block. But it still rocked his world when it came down. "My layoff was a spear aimed at my identity, my relationship network, and my family's livelihood," he said. "And so it temporarily broke me up."

With donations down, the organization decided in November 2008 to cut staff and terminate two hundred employees right before the holidays. Steve was a staff researcher, a quiet, studious man for whom principle is everything. Now, as the father of eight—including seven still at home, ages 13 through 19—Steve had special cause for concern. It drove him to his knees—and to prayerful consideration of just who he was as a Christian husband, father, and provider.

"I realized I was never the primary provider for my family," he said. "Just as Jesus says we have only *one* Father—and He resides in heaven—likewise we really only have *one* Provider. I'd have to go back to my sophomore year in high school to recall a Christmas where I didn't have a paycheck. During that time, I had for a long time expressed to others, 'Our security is not in a front-door lock or a paycheck'—and now God was asking me, 'Am I that same Secure Provider and Protector—or not?'"

"I'd have to go back to my sophomore year in high school to recall a Christmas where I didn't have a paycheck."

Steve and his wife, LauraLee, also found support in the body of Christ. "For several months, our friends, family, and fellow church members have rallied around us with occasional checks," he said. "We haven't been too prideful to go to our church's food pantry three times a month."

He also found ways to supplement unemployment insurance with part-time work as a football referee and softball umpire. Steve's ultimate new direction may be one that few people ever consider—working for another Christian ministry in a job requiring the employee to raise his own support from family, friends, and personal network.

"GOD, WHAT DO YOU WANT ME TO LEARN FROM THIS?"

Brian Clements had been in radio and TV broadcasting for twenty-nine years. Since being laid off, he has found some sporadic work as a cab driver and a substitute teacher while contemplating a complete career change, possibly in disaster management.

In terms of major life stressors, layoffs rank right up there on the short list along with death of a loved one, marriage and divorce, and physical illness. Brian got to experience several of those in a row. He was married to a fellow employee, in October 2007. The day after he returned to work from the honeymoon, he was informed that he had been selected to be laid off in a few months. "Of course, I was devastated, and so was my wife, Ellie," Brian said. "We prayed about it and tried to figure out what to do. Each month came and an extension was added, and it really did help my morale. I tried to keep a happy face, but a couple of people could see how I felt. I was angry. I would talk it out, and that would help. I even got in denial and tried to work even harder."

Meanwhile, Brian's father passed away. When he returned from the funeral, Brian noticed that the new schedule did not include him in the following week. It had taken nine months, but it had finally happened—he was through.

"It was one of the longest nine months I have ever experienced," said Brian. "The stress of it all, getting married, the death of my dad, being laid off. What really helped me, I think, was I was able to go to Germany and meet Ellie's folks for two weeks. That really relaxed me. I got to write in my prayer journal. On the way back, I had to fly back on my own while Ellie cared for her parents for a couple of weeks. Well, on the way back, I missed my connecting flight to Minneapolis and I was stuck in the Amsterdam airport for thirty hours. While I was waiting, I started asking God, 'What do you want me to learn from this?' I asked that for the entire thirty hours, and what I got was 'Stick with Me.'"

And that's what he's been doing ever since.

"THE ISOLATION CAN SEEM OVERWHELMING"

Mark Carlen had the dubious distinction of being laid off *twice* in close succession, first from his job in information technology. Unlike Steve and Brian, Mark was caught by total surprise. "I did not expect to be laid off at all, as my job was necessary to the regular operation of the organization," he said. "I don't think much thought was put into my dismissal, as someone had to be called in to cover my shift."

That was in October 2008. Then it happened again in January 2009. "Soon after the layoff, I found a contract position in Denver that I thought would keep me going through the economic downturn, but after a month on the job there, I was laid off again as the company let all of its contract workers go," said Mark. "I believe the second layoff hit me harder as it seemed the economy was sinking further and faster, and the breadth of opportunities was shriveling."

On the recommendation of an outplacement adviser, Mark started a support group for laid-off employees from his former organization. That's where I met Mark. We shared an appreciation for the value of relationship and fellowship that such groups provide in times of personal distress.

"The isolation one feels when looking for a job can seem overwhelming," said Mark. "So, having a group of friends who share the same problems and share ideas is an encouragement in itself. I think the loss of self-worth one feels when losing a job is directly related to the fact that they are no longer making a contribution to a larger group, but depending on others. While still dependent on others, the knowledge that I am making a contribution to someone else's well-being keeps my spirits high."

"MY BOSS AND I WERE A DEADLY MISMATCH"

Unlike some, it wasn't a market shakeout that cost Carol Bloom her job, but changes in the publishing industry certainly complicated her finding another position when things went south. Carol was publications director of an international honor society in education at a university town in Indiana. The clashes with her boss started almost immediately, only worsened over time, and eventually cost her her job.

"My management style was team coach; his was family patriarch," she said. "We were a deadly mismatch." Despite her department's growing success and national acclaim for its publications, Carol was fired in November 1995 after three and a half years. In her own words:

"The morning I was fired seemed set at a different speed. I arrived, I met my supervisor in his office, and within minutes I was typing up a resignation letter. If I refused to resign, I would receive no severance, only my current paycheck. If I resigned and signed a waiver that I would not take any legal action against my supervisor or the society, I would receive three months' severance. I hastily thought of my immediate need for survival and agreed to resign and sign the waiver. I have thought many times over whether I made the right decision, but my family would not have survived without my severance. I would not take further action, even filing for unemployment, because I respected the society and its leaders.

"After I turned in my resignation letter, I was given less than thirty minutes to call my husband (Bob), tell my staff, and leave

> **"The morning I was fired seemed set at a different speed."**

the premises. I would return three separate evenings to pack up my belongings, which had merged with the department's since I had no intention of ever leaving. My husband was speechless, although he and I had discussed reasons for my early meeting with my supervisor the night before. Telling my staff was surreal. I had known I could not work for my supervisor forever, but I always thought he would be the one to tire of his position and leave. I would never be the one to leave. My staff was outraged and supportive; they were not sure what to do or say. Neither was I.

"I drove home stunned. My thoughts raced: I was no longer with this honor society. I would no longer be producing its publications. I was thrown out as unsuitable. I was angry and crushed. Luckily, I had plans to go to my national social studies teachers' organization's annual conference the next day. I love to network because I love people, and rooming with an old friend and sharing my situation with empathetic colleagues calmed my worries and feelings of rejection and abandonment. I also saw several members of the honor society, who were incredulous at my fate and encouraging that I would land on my feet soon.

"But where would I land? What did I want to do? I had never planned to leave. Should I return to textbook publishing? Classroom teaching? Should we move to another city? My husband was up for a promotion to management, and neither of us relished moving again. I had not applied for a teaching license when we moved to this new state, so I could not teach or substitute, and I dreaded the corporate politics of the textbook publishing world. I knew I wanted to stay in publishing and preferably educational publishing."

The problem was a shrinking job market, as larger publishers continued to devour smaller ones. "With barely a handful of textbook publishers remaining," said Carol, "in-house staffs have shrunk significantly, and editorial management positions, which I would covet, would be few, very competitive, and centered in New York, Boston, or San Francisco, where our teenaged daughter's schooling and the cost of living would be concerns."

Her solution would have to involve the same independent-mindedness that had gotten her into trouble in the first place.

And if this is all just a bit discouraging, if not depressing, stay tuned. That's not the end of the story.

3

STARTING
OVER

Steve Kipp didn't wait to initiate the healing process. Before any bitterness could take root, he immediately sent an e-mail note of thanks and appreciation to the senior vice president for his division, who was out of the office when the ax fell but who would have had to sign off, at least, on Steve's termination. "I honestly had no bitterness toward my employers," Steve said. "Plus, I could honestly say, 'I'm glad it's me and not others.'" And that from a father of eight.

Not that there wasn't pain. But even that Steve turned into a learning experience: "Beware of the Rebound Response!" He explained:

"Within less than a month, my lingering temptation was to try to rebound into an immediate part-time church ministry position. It would at least 'save a little face,' show my coworkers that another ministry still considered me 'of value.' When you're over fifty, as the bulk of unemployed are growing to be, the common question seems to be 'Am I still of value to employers?'"

A curt rejection from that church was a good reality check to watch where he was trying to get life. Steve also had to fight a tendency to withdraw into himself and become less available relationally and emotionally to his family at the very time when they needed him more and he could be there physically as never before. But Steve is the kind of guy who could probably draw deep life lessons from things most people wouldn't even notice. So I asked him to share some of the lessons he's been learning from unemployment.

"Don't let the paycheck define your work/service in the Lord," he said. "Otherwise, it's not 'in the Lord,' is it? It's 'in yourself.'"

Steve cited something he had written in his personal journal five days after the layoff: "Don't be paralyzed by the monumental task before us." A "monument," he noted, is usually built of rock. "And in times of challenges, we need to see what rocks serve as our foundation." Things may not always be what they appear to the natural man. Steve tries, for example, to take the more biblical view of his large family as an asset—a full quiver (Psalm 127:5)—rather than a liability, i.e., mouths to be fed. And again, God as the true Provider.

He also prefers to view trials as good preparation for the future, like strength training. *Crisis*, Steve points out, in *koine* (New Testament) Greek means "judgment." "Enduring crises now," he said, "is one way God prepares us for the major one awaiting us all."

With Steve's degree of faith and spiritual vision, he seems to be a natural for a future ministry position that requires him to raise his own support.

Brian Clements has been using this life interruption to pursue training in an area of lifelong interest to him—emergency management. He found that the federal government has a bevy of free training modules online, and he has been working his way through all of them. As a member of the group of ex-employees, he had the opportunity to critique the original version of this book, *Reinventing Your Career*, which he found helpful. It helped him, he said, face the unpleasant reality that he may be compelled to accept a career change, especially in light of a chronic hearing problem that has been a challenge in the broadcast business.

It's up to God where He wants me. I have to find the doors that open and walk in.

"Where will this take me and where will I end up?" said Brian. "I don't know. It's up to God where He wants me. I have to find the doors that open and walk in."

IF YOU CAN'T GET A JOB, MAKE ONE

Even with his back against the wall, Mark Carlen is about as sanguine as they come—enterprising, too. Maybe that's a by-product of a career that's included restaurant management and swimming pool service and repair, among other things. "I have generally worked a total of fifty to sixty hours a week at one or two jobs," he told me. He's also one of those people who's been able to make a modest income on the side reselling goods of all kinds on eBay and Craigslist.

Mark has been using his layoff time for additional training toward IT certification in computer systems management. But that may not be the final destination. Ultimately, he has some entrepreneurial ideas for businesses he'd like to start once he's back on his feet financially.

"One great thing about America," he said, "is that if you can't get a job, you can make one."

Now let's see how Carol, our editor, made out.

● ● ●

> **"Being very social, I feared that home would isolate me from human contact."**
> **—Carol**

After taking a personal self-inventory, Carol Bloom's solution was to form her own venture, a full-service editorial company called Bloom Ink Publishing Professionals. "Because I loved project management, I could take on planning and creating a book, publication, annual report, or brochure from initial concept to final printed product," she said. Bloom Ink services would include copyediting, writing, proofreading, manuscript analysis, publication evaluation, consulting, and publications/print project management.

"Several of my friends who had left the textbook publisher were succeeding as independent contractors," she said. "So I interviewed them about the ups and downs of being in business for themselves. I learned that the flow of work was often feast and famine and that publishers paid better than the development houses often employed by publishers to handle editorial and production stages of teacher materials. Every freelancer I spoke to mentioned cash flow concerns—clients taking up to twelve weeks to pay for freelance services.

"Unlike me, most of these women loved the solitude of home as a workplace. Being very social and extroverted, I feared that home would isolate me from human contact and loneliness would consume me. And indeed, after I had decided to take the risk of owning my own business, I did fight loneliness for the first two months."

The experience also resulted in some self-discovery. Still dealing with her own troubled emotions, Carol sought counseling.

"It has helped me immensely," she said of the counseling. "The hurt, anger, and loneliness dissipated as I talked about my feelings in being fired and its aftermath. I learned that the environment at the office was dysfunctional and the behavior of my supervisor resembled that of an alcoholic father. The employees were his children, each trying to stay out of his way, glad not to gain his attention for fear it would be a negative experience. When any one of us was in his favor, we enjoyed it cautiously, knowing we would soon enough be on the outs. By being direct and confrontational when a problem surfaced, I was forcing him to look at reality instead of the world he preferred to configure for us all.

"Because I was not willing to be a player in his charade, despite his respect for my abilities, with time he could no longer permit me to be a part of the family. Now knowing better how such a climate is maintained by a controlling person, I was better able to accept that I had little control over changing the environment, which I feared was my failing, and that it was best for my health and sanity that I was no longer a part of that office."

Bloom Ink did indeed take flight, for a while. But it wasn't long before Carol discovered the risks and hazards too often encountered by the entrepreneur. It eventually led her back into fulltime employment for another organization. But in the spring of 1996, she was exhilarated to land a major project with one of the top textbook publishers in the country for junior and senior high school texts. She went out and hired two writers, a graphic designer, and a photo editor. Everything went fine and on time, including the first of three remittances from the publishers. And then the money stopped coming.

"Management had no intention to cut the check until the year ended."

Repeated calls to the publisher brought only the same repeated promises that it was in the works—but it wasn't. "Unbeknownst to me, the company was not paying any of its independent contractors in the fall so its balance sheet was impressive for the British publishing company that was purchasing it," Carol said. "I learned what risk was all about as I tried to stay afloat financially. Management had no intention to cut the check until the year ended.

We nearly lost our house, and my competent team nearly quit working for me."

Bloom Ink would never undertake another textbook project, even though this first and last one won a regional award. "Recognition only slightly soothed my deep wounds," she said.

Carol tried a middle way—dividing her time between Bloom Ink and a part-time copywriting job with a local advertising agency in West Lafayette, Indiana. This did not turn out to be a very workable strategy. "I would learn in the morning when they needed me, and it became nearly impossible for me to take on freelance jobs because I never knew how many hours I could devote to a Bloom Ink job," she said.

Other troubles robbed Carol of her joy, resilience, and focus—death of her mother, a bad car accident that left her with chronic back pain, depression. In 2006 she went to work as a staff writer in an office of Purdue University. Carol turned sixty in June 2009, clearly full of regrets for what might have been in her frustrated attempt at self-employment. Yet, she has not stopped hoping and dreaming.

"I relish my limited time with my loving husband, who has worked second shift through nearly all of our thirty-eight years together," she said. "I may be at least six years away from the days of retirement and Social Security, and I pray that another opportunity that draws on my strongest skills presents itself soon, so I can once again be master of my own destiny."

4

THE WAVE
OF CHANGE

In Floyd Kemske's novel *Lifetime Employment*,
a couple of employees of a high-tech company
encounter the hero, Gene, on the elevator.

It doesn't take long to see this is not your typi-
cal elevator conversation about the weather. "We
want you to kill Larry," says one of them, referring
to the chief of information systems.

Gene is taken aback, but less than one might
expect. "I'll have to get back to you on that," he
says, edging away from the employees. The reader
wonders if Gene is just stalling or whether he first
has to do a cost/benefit analysis on Larry.

At this company, the employees literally climb
over the bodies of their coworkers to advance their
own careers. Permanent job security is just a shot
away for the victors. In a sense, the victims are
actually the first—and maybe the only ones for
sure—to achieve lifetime employment. It's just that
their lifetimes are somewhat shorter than the norm.

In another Kemske novel, *Virtual Boss*, a business firm has so decentralized that the only actual authority is a computer program—a bundle of interactive artificial intelligence software. It learns from its employee interactions and adapts its responses to facilitate peak performance from the myriad individual personalities. For one person, that may mean simple encouragement. For another, it may mean turning his life into a living hell. The virtual boss is more than willing to accommodate—and for some workers, hell it is.

And in *Human Resources*, Kemske pictures a corporate turnaround expert who comes to Biomethods, Inc., spouting all the latest jargon about "tearing down walls" and reengineering the corporation. Translation: Rip out an organization's guts, close down entire departments, and send longtime employees packing. So, that's fiction? In this case, the turnaround expert is also a vampire—a boss who figuratively and literally sucks the life out of employees. The vampire/boss, named Pierce, also guts a project seeking a cure for AIDS in favor of a different scheme to identify people's buying patterns by a blood test. Much better for the bottom line.

Kemske's novels would be good choices for a time capsule. Their satirically exaggerated picture of life in the waning months and years of the twentieth century would be a wonderful, though macabre, find for future archaeologists curious about today's phenomenon of dispensable workers and disposable people.

Except for the vampire, the Biomethods story is the all-too-familiar scenario of mass layoffs/firings that haunts today's headlines. So-called human resources are being consumed like cords of wood, veins of ore, and carloads of coal. And, like the old vilified strip mines, the landscape is left scarred and littered with the detritus of human lives—living, breathing people who can give plaintive interviews to the *New York Times* and whose cries can be heard on the nightly news.

REPURPOSED

The negatives of joblessness are easy to see.
Besides the obvious loss of income, there may be other losses:

sometimes the loss of a standard of living, loss of self-
esteem, even loss of a home or a mate. The divorce rate,
according to several studies, is as much as 50 percent
higher than the national average in families where one
earner, usually the man, has lost a job and cannot quickly
find an equivalent one.[1]

Truly, losing a job can ruin at least your day—maybe your year, maybe your life. Not so apparent are the gains. It takes special vision to see the benefits of job loss, but it can be done. Not all jobs are good for the soul; job loss does often lead to something much better down the road; there are ways to recover from the grief that accompanies job loss.

One afternoon I shared a seat on a bus with a woman whose job was to find new words for Webster's *New World Dictionary*. More accurately, the object of her search was neologisms, which include not just new words, but also new meanings for old words and compounds of old words used in new ways. Computer technology has given rise to many of these—e.g., *network, reboot, surf, web, software, database*. This woman said the business world, because of upheaval in the workplace, also has been a fertile field for neologisms—*downsizing, outsourcing, telecommuting, reengineering*.

I was pleased to be able to give her a new one she had not heard that derived from both the computer and business realms—*repurposing*. I had heard it from a friend who worked for a local

Not all jobs are good for the soul; job loss does often lead to something much better down the road.

computer retailer and had garnered a national reputation of sorts as an expert communicator on the subject of digital video—which in 1996 I'd originally termed "a mushrooming field that may someday be as familiar to the average consumer as microwaves and fax machines." (YouTube was years away from being a gleam in anyone's eye.) One day he informed me that he had been "repurposed." He explained that, just as software designed for one application can be modified and converted to another application, so had he been repurposed from working with this new digital video technology to selling service contracts to computer customers.

This was not a happy occasion. He spent the weekend in bed, immobilized by depression. Months later, he was still working in the same place, tormented by the desire to leave, but kept in check by the fear of risking the little that he still had to find something better, as well as the remote possibility that things would someday return to normal at his current job. I almost wished that he would be fired, as I had been, so he could get on with life.

For believers, our responses to life's unhappy surprises can and should be "more than a feeling."

For believers, our responses to life's unhappy surprises can and should be "more than a feeling." We can begin to understand how the apostle Paul could use such an apparent contradiction as "sorrowful, yet always rejoicing" in referring to a Christian's attitude through hardships (2 Corinthians 6:10). Not only is this nonsense to the worldly mind, but it refers to a strength of character that even believers can only realize through adversity. I know this is for real, for I have actually seen it in believers like Steve Kipp.

"I'm embracing the reality that God hasn't promised us hard-free times or a 'suffering lite' brand of Christianity," said Steve in the midst of his unemployment. "But He *has* promised to be there with us through every moment. Am I going to tap into His limitless resources or just try to 'scrape' by on my own puny production?

My Bible doesn't know the word 'coping.' It only knows being an 'Overcomer'" (Revelation 2–3).

Steve said reading a commentary by theologian Matthew Henry while out of work threw a whole new light on the meaning of "employment" for him. Our spirits, Henry wrote, are to be *employed* in prayer and in the service of God. "It reinforced within me that my 'employment' in God's service wasn't dependent on a paycheck," he said. "My prayer life, my devotional life, my worship life were intended for 24/7 employable service—in which I was available for *deployment* by God for service to Him and others."

For the believer, Matthew 6:33 should be more than a Christian cliché or a plaque on the wall: "But seek first his kingdom and his righteousness, and all these things will be given to you as well." In the Sermon on the Mount, by "these things" Jesus was referring to the necessities of life—food, clothing, shelter. Steve is one believer determined to take God at His word and to live out this promise.

This perspective can be truly revolutionary in our lives. Being out of work—and without "visible means of support"—can be an opportunity to experience the supernatural, to be refined in the fire, to develop Christlike character, and to see what amazing new things God may have in store for us. It can be an opportunity for us to be divinely *repurposed*.

WORKAHOLICS AND CODEPENDENTS

There's another neologism from the 1990s: *Job lock.* Usually, it refers to the immobilization related to the fear of losing employment benefits—especially health insurance, which is expensive under any circumstances, but for some people with medical problems it cannot be purchased at any price. But the term is also applicable when a life becomes so totally dependent upon a job that it has become a veritable puppet master.

There are thousands of people like this, probably millions. It's a sickness that has become endemic to entire organizations themselves, according to Anne Wilson Schaef and Diane Fassel, authors of *The Addictive Organization*. They define an addiction as anything we feel we have to lie about and that we're not willing to give up to make our lives fuller and healthier. It's surely no accident that America's most socially acceptable addiction has nothing to do with pills or booze. It's called "workaholism."

Everyone knows the familiar scenario of the family torn apart by an alcoholic or substance abuser whose erratic, even destructive, behavior keeps other members of the family in a constant terrorized state. It's the scenario that has given rise to another neologism—*codependency*. Simply put, people who subordinate their own feelings and needs in order to mediate the behavior of an alcoholic, for example, in a very real sense also share the alcoholic's addiction; they are codependent.

But by the same token, how many would recognize the same pattern in the workplace? Schaef and Fassel say these real-life scenarios are identical to the patterns observed in ACOAs—adult children of alcoholics. In *The Addictive Organization*, one woman described a father who was completely consumed by his work:

> We rarely saw him. Sometimes he stayed in the city overnight or on big projects he would be gone for weeks at a time. Work was the overriding excuse for everything, family celebrations, plans, and vacations all bowed to the demands of work. We could never count on anything. My father married his work and it had the excitement of a mistress. I don't think my mother or our family were ever second place in my father's life, I believe for him we didn't exist at all. I grew up spending inordinate amounts of time thinking about my father, yet never really knowing him. I hate him for this and I miss him deeply.[2]

There may be inner reasons for that kind of behavior that go back to family relationship dynamics. The workplace—

dysfunctional as it may be—can repre-
sent a refuge for the workaholic, who
is better at work than he is at rela-
tionships. The addiction is subtle, but
strong. Our boss may become a
surrogate parent, according to Schaef
and Fassel, to fulfill needs that were
never met at home—attention, encour-
agement, approval. Denial comes in when we
hide from ourselves the truth that, just as with the
false promise of drugs, we will never be able to get what
we want in the end. Nevertheless, we maintain the fiction that
fulfillment lies just around the corner, if we only work a little
harder, a little longer. And when we fail, we at least look heroic
to others—a hard worker, maybe even a martyr.

What happens when the organization revokes your membership and says, "Your services are no longer required"?

It's a scary thought that in many organizations the "best"
employees often come from the most dysfunctional homes. These
are the ones, according to Schaef and Fassel, who are willing to
subordinate their own needs and "let the company become their
family." Thus, they are willing to do whatever it takes—longer
hours, more responsibilities—just to maintain acceptance by the
organization. No burden is too heavy; no sacrifice is too great.
The rest of us, out of economic necessity, may find ourselves
forced to play along and get sucked into the same dynamics.
We've become codependent.

It's scary for a couple of reasons. At the root, this hold on
people's lives—unquestioning attachment to an organization that
defines our very identity—is little different from the dynamics
of Jonestown, Waco's Branch Davidians, and other cults, though
the outward goals may be more benign or, at least, less contro-
versial. The other scary question is: What happens when the
organization revokes your membership and says, "Your services
are no longer required"?

No wonder people are devastated by layoffs/firings—some

much more than others. The psychic blow can be crushing when it threatens the core of their being.

David Noer, in *Healing the Wounds*, wrote: "People who are organizationally codependent have enabled the system to control their sense of worth and self-esteem at the same time that they invest tremendous energy attempting to control the system. . . . If who you are is where you work, what are you if you lose your job?"[3]

SICK SURVIVORS

Or, for that matter, who are you when other heads start rolling and yours is spared from the chopping block? Not necessarily that much better off. That's why Noer coined the term "layoff survivor sickness" for those left behind but definitely not unaffected.

"Words commonly used to describe the symptoms of layoff survivor sickness," wrote Noer, "are anger, depression, fear, distrust, and guilt. People with survivor sickness have often been described as having a reduced desire to take risks, a lowered commitment to the job, and a lack of spontaneity."[4]

As either a victim or survivor, there's anger and shame that can be destructive if acted out or turned inward and allowed to harden into bitterness and resentment. The results can be incapacitating at a time when initiative, energy, and resilience are needed the most. But that's exactly what happens when those feelings get stuffed, which is often the strategy of choice among people who want to show the world a stiff upper lip.

Why should layoff/firing survivors suffer similar repercussions as the victims? It seems to defy common sense. Some counselors refer to this process in terms of the Lifegiver Principle, in which the Lifegiver can be a parent, an employer, or some other figure of significance who can impact our well-being, such as a spouse in a codependent relationship. An analogy would be to the family in divorce whose children struggle with feelings of guilt, as if they had been somehow responsible for the marital split. The Lifegiver cannot be wrong; so it must be me, goes the reasoning. Similarly, says Noer, "There is a sense that you have done something wrong if you get laid off."[5]

The problem with internalizing—stuffing feelings—is they don't just disappear; they fester under cover. King Solomon said three thousand years ago, "A cheerful heart is good medicine, but a crushed spirit dries up the bones" (Proverbs 17:22). That's where people of faith have a leg up on others, if they have another source of life from which to draw—the ultimate Lifegiver—so the loss of a job does not mean loss of identity, meaning, and self-worth. Unemployment is not a total loss if out of it comes a new experience in self-knowledge or even a spiritual awakening, as often happens to a person after the death of a loved one.

It took an unemployment crisis . . . to make me realize I had a problem with my priorities.

For me, it took an employment crisis—and the resulting feelings of despair and depression—to make me realize that I had a problem with my priorities. In the scheme of things—God, family, job—I had unwittingly elevated my career out of reasonable proportion. Solomon, I think, would have called it idolatry.

GRIEVING YOUR LOSSES

Part of reinventing your career is to bring closure to the anger, fear, and grief you feel. The crushed spirit must be attended to, even if it means allowing the untidiness of spilled emotions. That may mean crying or even raging—for a season. That may seem awkward or unnatural, but if you're frozen in inactivity or despair, that's a sure sign of unfinished emotional business. King Solomon said there is a time for everything, including "a time to weep and a time to laugh, a time to mourn and a time to dance" (Ecclesiastes 3:4). Release also can involve talking things through with a trusted partner, friend, spouse, or support group. If you have none of the above, that in itself is a problem that needs to be addressed. Your network is too small—or too shallow.

The words of Baltasar Gracián, the seventeenth-century Spanish Jesuit sage, are still apropos more than three hundred years later:

> There is gratification in sharing joyful events and an advantage to partnership. More important is to discover someone to help shoulder your misfortunes. The hour of danger, the shadow of distress, will seem less forbidding with someone at your side. . . . This explains why the intelligent physician, having missed the cure, does not miss calling another, who under the name of consultant helps him carry the coffin. Divide with another your burdens and your sorrows. For misfortune, always difficult, is doubly unbearable to him who stands alone.[6]

We live in an age when many people gnash their teeth at the promotions, raises, and other successes of their associates or even take secret pleasure in their misfortune—what the Germans call *Schadenfreude*. But the apostle Paul set a higher standard: "Rejoice with those who rejoice; mourn with those who mourn" (Romans 12:15). That is the kind of friend you need, someone who can share your pain. Paul calls God Himself "the Father of compassion and the God of all comfort, who comforts us in all our troubles, so that we can comfort those in any trouble with the comfort we ourselves have received from God" (2 Corinthians 1:3–4). Notice how the comforting process makes us partakers of the divine.

But the greatest resistance to breaking the emotional logjam may come from within. Thomas Gordon, an expert in organizational psychology, says that from our earliest years we are conditioned to regard feelings almost as dangerous enemies.

This attitude is embedded in numerous messages: "Don't feel bad. . . . Swallow your pride. . . . Hold your temper. . . . Bite your tongue." In *Leadership Effectiveness Training*, Gordon wrote years ago that there is a "strong ban" in the workplace on such feelings as irritation, anger, frustration, disappointment, hurt, fear, futility, despair, hate, bitterness, and discouragement. There is little reason to doubt that such tendencies would carry over into unemployment.

"While experiencing such feelings is not unhealthy, repressing them is," according to Gordon. "Continually bottling up your feelings is very definitely 'hazardous to your health' and can ultimately cause ulcers, headaches, heartburn, high blood pressure, spastic colon, or any number of other psychosomatic problems. Repressed feelings can also reduce your effectiveness just by distracting you from your work."[7]

And if you are out of a job, your work is finding a job—or reinventing your career.

Cliff Hakim, a career consultant, recommends an exercise called storytelling that can have both immediate and long-term benefits. Catharsis—giving vent to negative emotions—and the closure that comes from sharing the account of your career trials and tribulations can bring welcome relief to the soul. It can also help regroup your forces for a new game on life's chessboard. Storytelling, according to Hakim in *When You Lose Your Job*, involves "talking with people who will listen, not offer judgments, about your loss, fears, and abilities. By telling your story, you'll have the opportunity to share your feelings, then name them. Second, you can filter out what you do and don't want to share with a potential employer."[8]

It's important to develop a "no sour grapes" explanation of your job loss, which should be part of this exercise. Above all,

Employment insecurity may not be a temporary situation; it may become a way of life.

lay the facts to rest and face the truth fully. Noer says many strug-
gling employees have to face the fact that they may be "acting out
a play that closed long ago." Denial must stop. Employment in-
security may not be a temporary situation; it may become a way
of life. There may be more than one job loss in the average
worker's future. Reality, unpalatable as it can be, must be faced.[9]

RIDING THE EMOTIONAL ROLLER COASTER

Flash back to very similar times in 1996 at the Cuyahoga
County Reemployment Services Center in Cleveland: The aver-
age job seeker had been out of work for six months with unem-
ployment insurance about to run out, and things were getting
very serious. Some had been going through the motions without
much progress. Some were paralyzed by inaction. Many of them
had unfinished business. Oftentimes, they hadn't grieved their
loss yet.

Robert E. Paponetti, then center director, said there's a cor-
relation with the classic grief process in studies of death and
dying. But not everybody is ready to accept the idea right away.
Some, even job placement workers, tend to regard the concept as
a little too much like pop psychology. Until, that is, they see it for
themselves directly.

"When the program was first set up," said Paponetti, "this
piece was in there and some of our job developers, who are on the
back end, who are really working hard to get jobs, they kind of
scoffed at this whole emotional part—'That's touchy-feely, it's
just slowing down the whole process.' So, I said, let's try to cir-
cumvent that. We will identify people who, the day they come in,
if they feel like they're ready and we think they are ready, we will
have them go right into the next process, *Learning How to Get a
Job*, which we tried for a couple weeks.

"What was happening, our instructors who were teaching
the employability stuff said, 'You know, we are spending more
time talking about the actual job of looking for a job. They need

to go back and get this piece. They have to go back and talk about it and vent and bring it to a closure.' "

Rick Crow handled this issue by walking counselees through a graphical roller coaster, "The Wave of Change," modeled on the grief process. Then they talked about their feelings in small groups. Crow said people who have been unable to open up to anyone else, including close family members, find it natural, if not easy, to do so among others who have had the same experience. And, in doing so, they find some release, especially from the feeling of isolation, that "I'm the only one in this boat."

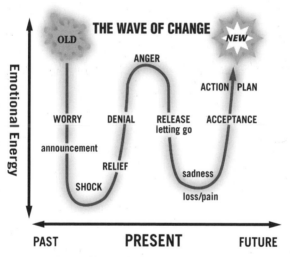

Courtesy of Cuyahoga County Reemployment Services Center

In the typical layoff/firing scenario, the emotional roller coaster starts with worry, as rumors swirl that an ax is about to fall. It is followed by shock, with the actual announcement of jobs being cut, a letdown in terms of emotional energy. Ironically, the next reaction is relief, as the fear of the unknown is dispelled by naked reality. Everyone now knows who must take the long walk off the short plank. That particular anxiety is over. The devil that we know is preferable to the one we don't know.

Next on the roller-coaster ride comes denial, as the mind throws up defenses against the external threat to its security. "No!" it cries. "It can't be. There must be some mistake." The next reaction is anger, as reality sinks in and the sense of outrage against the violation builds. But anger cannot sustain itself forever, and eventually there is a release, as the emotion spends itself and the person begins to let go, through exhaustion if nothing else. In emotional terms, this is the second trough as the wave of loss and pain overwhelms us.

At last, there is another upswing that puts the wave of change behind us, as we reach an acceptance of the unchangeable circumstance and begin to put it behind us. This is the point where we develop our action plan for getting on with the rest of our life. That might mean snapping out of the defeat mode, updating the résumé, and starting to knock on doors. Or it might mean just the opposite—hanging up the job search and going into business for oneself.

Whatever the case, the time for pity parties is over; the time for action has come.

5

AT THE
CORE

How does the jobless person manage—let alone
master—the change that's been forced upon him?

Ironically, much of the answer may be found
within the very organizations that have been gener-
ating all of this joblessness in the first place. Faced
with challenges to their very survival in a world of
global competition and rapid technological change,
business organizations have been forced to reinvent
themselves in a couple of key ways—discovering a
sense of purpose or mission and focusing on their
core competencies. Individuals will have to do much
the same thing to reinvent their own careers and
survive the threats to their economic survival.

DISCOVERING PURPOSE

David Noer's prescription is detachment—letting go—and connecting to a core purpose: "Each person must determine his or her unique purpose in life."[1] If this language sounds familiar, it's much the same talk emanating from the executive suites these days in regard to the large organization. Now everybody is writing mission statements, vision statements, and statements of purpose.

The late W. Edwards Deming, a main pillar of the quality movement through his Total Quality Management system, brought the organizational mission to the forefront of attention in the world of business management. Significantly, the very first of his fourteen famous TQM principles exhorts organizations to create "constancy of purpose" for products and services. This is trickier than it sounds; it requires raising the sights and taking the long view.

At the turn of the nineteenth century there were two very different buggy whip-makers. The first one committed itself to making the best buggy whips on the market. The second one devoted itself to transportation. Today, the first one is history. The second one is making automotive carburetors.

A number of automakers in the early 1900s started out as bicycle companies that were willing to reinvent themselves. Motorola purposed to create a superior, repairable product, but it lost its TV market to foreign competitors who could make superior products that didn't need repair. Whether it's a buggy whip company, a bicycle maker, an automaker, or an electronics manufacturer, the principle is the same: It not only has to invent new products and services; it has to reinvent itself.

The same is true for individuals. If you don't know where you're headed, someone said, you may end up where you don't want to be. Images abound: the gasping pilgrim clawing his

If you don't know where you're headed, someone said, you may end up where you don't want to be.

way to a Himalayan summit in anxious search of truths about the meaning of life; the sidewalk derelict huddled over a steam heat grate, devoid of any direction in life; the business professional climbing the career ladder, only to find it's leaning against the wrong building.

As King Solomon once said: "The purposes of a man's heart are deep waters, but a man of understanding draws them out" (Proverbs 20:5).

Counselors, therapists, and others who study human behavior have identified several major common denominators as core personal needs. The classic one in Psychology 101 texts is Abraham Maslow's hierarchy of needs. Higher up the ladder after the basic physiological needs (food, shelter, and so on) and physical safety are the more interpersonal drives—acceptance, esteem, and self-actualization. Other authors have expressed similar principles in slightly different terms, such as relationship, integrity, and impact.

Relationship involves our social needs, which include being affirmed as a person with worth and dignity as a valued member of a larger whole, even if it's only a partnership of two. Integrity relates to issues of fairness, justice, honesty, and the need for equitable and forthright treatment in school, work, politics, or any other organization, no matter the size. For managers, the issues will involve the credibility of their leadership in terms of practicing what they preach.

Impact is sometimes called significant purpose. It involves making a contribution, making a difference, standing at the plate and getting a hit. In *Understanding People*, psychologist Lawrence J. Crabb Jr., defined impact as "a desire to be adequate for a meaningful task, a desire to know that we are capable of taking hold of our world and doing something valuable and well."[2]

The first time I ever saw a battery-powered hand drill was decades ago in one of the Old Man's Cave parks in southern Ohio. It was in the hands of a man intent on inscribing his name upon a boulder located on a scenic overlook. Outraged, my wife sought out a park ranger after we returned to our camp. The ranger assured her that the problem had already been dealt with. Some young "hippie" types, similarly outraged, had come upon the man and made a citizen's arrest. "But people would be able to read my name for a hundred years!" the man reportedly exclaimed as he was served his citation.

Our misguided Michelangelo illustrated dramatically, if in a less than socially acceptable manner, that the desire for impact on our world is a deep, primal need. Is there any question how directly impact applies to the workplace? "We want to know that we are capable of doing a job that needs to be done," wrote Crabb. "We want to leave a mark on our world, a real and enduring difference that matters."[3]

If impact—or significant purpose—is such a driving force, why wouldn't an individual as much as a big corporation need a personal statement of purpose? Perry Pascarella and Mark A. Frohman described in *The Purpose-Driven Organization* the corporate benefits such an exercise provides—direction, focus, policy, meaning, challenge, and passion. "All of us want to be more than a number at work," they wrote. "We want our work to enhance our self-respect and satisfy our desire to achieve. In short, we want our work to provide meaning for us. A purpose statement provides meaning by defining something greater to relate to than the job itself. It offers a broader context in which to fit our daily work."[4]

Purpose is even more applicable to the jobless individual looking to get back into the race. James Collins and Jerry Porras, authors of *Built to Last: Successful Habits of Visionary Companies*, described purpose as a "guiding star" to reestablish direction and a reason for organizational (or personal) existence. It gives meaning to work and something to believe in. Where there is no clear overall aim, the results can be disasterous—as with U.S. strategy in Vietnam, where lack of an overall aim was said to be one of the downfalls of the war effort.

FOCUSING ON THE CORE

Before addressing the personal statement of purpose, it would be good to consider some further dimensions of organizational mission. In their six-year study of long-lasting, visionary companies, Collins and Porras focused on what they called "core ideology," which consists of core values plus purpose. Core values comprise the organization's basic tenets and guiding principles. Purpose is defined as "the organization's fundamental reasons for existence beyond just making money."[5]

A poor purpose statement for Walt Disney, for example, would have been: "We exist to make cartoons for kids," having little power to motivate anyone for very long, according to Collins and Porras. Fortunately, Disney did better than that: "To bring happiness to millions" and to celebrate, nurture, and promulgate "wholesome American values." These values include fanatical attention to consistency and detail and continuous progress via creativity, dreams, and imagination.[6]

Sometimes values are expressed in terms of vision, and some organizations craft both a mission and a vision statement. One such organization is one of America's largest employers, the Hospital Corporation of America (formerly Columbia/HCA Healthcare Corp.), the largest private operator of health-care facilities in the world. Its mission: "We are committed to the care and improvement of human life. In recognition of this commitment, we strive to deliver high quality, cost-effective healthcare in the communities we serve." Its vision (at one point, at least): "To work with employees and physicians to build a company that is focused on the well-being of people, that is patient oriented, that offers the most advanced technology and information systems, that is financially sound, and that is synonymous with quality, cost-effective healthcare."

America's hospitals provide vivid examples of one of the forces behind the "flattening" of organizations and the loss of jobs—outsourcing. Historically, hospitals as community institutions have tried to be full-service operations with their own employees staffing a wide range of departments from laundry to food service to power plants to information systems. This self-sufficiency has all but ended in recent years as financial pressures have forced hospitals to reduce head counts, focus on what they can do best, and farm out the rest to other organizations that could provide those services with greater quality and economy. Hospitals found themselves forced to narrow their focus to their core competencies— direct health care services. Groundskeeping, housekeeping, and security are more properly the core competencies of landscape, cleaning, and security firms.

This is the same thing the public sector has been discovering in governmental operations down to the level of townships that farm out trash hauling. There it's called "privatizing." But it's the same difference—contracting out to those who are the best and most efficient providers of those services. And it's the same principle employed by commercial enterprises in a form called "niche marketing," in which a specialty food company, for example, might specialize in imported fish from South America because it has found a very specific place in the market where it can excel and dominate.

And increasingly, individuals must do much the same thing in their own personal careers.

IDEAS ON PAPER, WORDS IN PRINT

Some of the best advice I got when I decided to try self-employment was to narrow my focus in terms of the services I would offer to the public. I called my one-man band Adams Business Communications (ABC). I knew I would be offering writing, editing, and public relations services, but I also considered adding videography to the portfolio. With an eye to the future, I hoped to diversify my communications offerings beyond the printed word.

But Tony, a church friend and chief financial officer for a large company, asked a few challenging questions. Did I have experience with video? Was I particularly technically minded? No, I had to answer in each case. My core competencies were really writing, editing, and public relations. "Then," said Tony, "stick with those and even narrow them further to a niche you can dominate by being the best in that area so that people will think of you when they think of that service. If you want to work in the video area, find a good specialist and form a strategic alliance," he said.

I soon discovered the wisdom of that approach. Through my network of contacts after sixteen years in the same city, I was able to find opportunities as an independent contractor helping out PR agencies with special projects and as a freelance business writer. The fact that I had published a couple of novels helped convince me—my core competency was writing, especially on business topics and health care. I decided to make that my stock-in-trade and came up with a slogan that I put on my business cards: *Ideas on Paper, Words in Print.*

A number of observations began to jell in my mind. I began to realize that I really worked best on my own rather than as part of a team or under an authoritarian structure. I was strongly self-directed and actually enjoyed intensely creative projects under my own management. The words of my late father, a small businessman, when we had once discussed my journalism career came back to me: "Well, Son, nobody gets rich working for somebody else." At the time, the words had meant little to me because I was more of an idealist than a materialist. "Getting rich" to me was about as attractive an idea as getting old.

When I really thought about it, I'd always disliked being an employee.

But now I realized that it didn't necessarily have to mean having a lot of money. For me, a "rich" life might be simply having economic independence, maybe finding out if I could run my own business. When I really thought about it, I'd always disliked being an employee. I had no aversion to work, but having to report five days a week at prescribed hours to a specific place to receive instructions felt all too much like indentured servitude. But I had never given these feelings much thought. If I had, I probably would have figured this was simply the way things were and I was wrong to feel that way.

My statement of purpose, had I actually written it out at that point, would have been something like this: *I am committed to working as an independent contractor on projects of my choosing involving ideas on paper and words in print. As a writer and editor, I value the self-direction, independence, and creative satisfaction of the writing process itself. I am not a natural organization-climber nor administrator; my role within an organization would more naturally be as a teacher, trainer, or communicator.*

Here is a fine but important point. It was not that I couldn't function as a supervisor. In fact, I had worked as an assistant city editor of a large metropolitan newspaper for a number of years, supervising reporters. But was that my core competency? Probably not. I could do it adequately, but never as effectively as I could do the work of a writer. The reality is that in today's competitive times neither organizations nor individuals can afford to play anything but their strongest suit. How many people are getting stressed out and burned out trying to play roles that are not genuinely their own? Too many, no doubt.

Confusion here can be fatal. Without understanding your core competencies, it is even harder to identify your life mission, vision, and purpose. In the church, we say if you want to know God's plan for your life, look at your gifts—another way of saying core competencies. If you don't have a gift for public speaking and don't like working with people, for example, it's not likely you're being called to the ministry.

It also needs to be *your* mission and vision, not someone else's expectations. As an early member of the baby boom generation, I was one of the square pegs that tried to fit into the round holes of science and technology in the wake of the Sputnik challenge. There was a rampant fear in the late 1950s and early 1960s that the United States would lose out to the Soviets in the technology race unless America mounted a crash effort among its schoolchildren to produce more scientists and technicians by directing them into advanced science and math programs. It took me a few years in college to unlearn this programming and, through personal failures, to discover that my real gifts were in an entirely different area.

Finding a niche first involves self-knowledge, knowing your gifts.

What about you? Do you know what your real gifts are? If you were to write your own personal mission statement, what would it say?

6

THE JOURNEY
OF SELF-DISCOVERY

What is a career? W*ebster's New World Dictionary*
defines it as "one's progress through life in a partic-
ular vocation." The word originally meant a race
course. In fact, the word *car* is a linguistic relative.
The verb "to career" means "to move at full speed;
to rush wildly," according to Webster's. In addition
to the idea of a race there is something else: There
is an assumption that the natural state is one
vocation—literally, "calling"—per person.
For life.

As we have seen, however, those days are gone,
perhaps forever. No more than we would expect to
drive the same car all our lives can we expect life-
time employment or even a lifetime career. The
marketplace is changing too rapidly. In that case,
what good are all our talents and gifts, innately fixed
as they are?

Too many years ago in college, I had a part-time job in the university's Office Services department, operating an Addressograph machine (does anybody today even know what that is?). This was the low-tech device with trays of metal plates that was once used to stamp names and addresses on outgoing materials to an organization's mailing list, in this case alumni and financial supporters. Considering what happened to that technology in subsequent years, it was good that I continued my studies. It was not to be a skill I could ever fall back on. Today, Addressograph operators have about as much calling as keypunchers or Linotypists in the era of modern computers and electronic cold-type printing.

Today, when jobs and job descriptions change faster than Paris fashions, career counselors speak in terms of transferable skills. For machine operators forced to change horses in mid-career, transferable skills might include an interest in operating precision equipment, good hand-eye coordination and mechanical ability, and a tolerance for long periods of performing routine tasks repetitively.

Transferable skills are different from job content skills, which are the more obvious skills peculiar to a specific job, such as measuring, cutting, and hammering for a carpenter. As the name implies, transferable skills can be transferred from one job—or one career—to another, such as instructing others, managing money, managing people, meeting deadlines, meeting with the public, negotiating, organizing/managing projects, public speaking, and written communications skills. Other transferable skills, based on a listing from the Cuyahoga County Reemployment Services Center:

- **Dealing with things**—assembling, building, constructing, repairing, driving, manual tasks, inspecting, operating
- **Dealing with data**—checking, classifying, comparing, compiling, counting, evaluating, investigating, recording, locating, observing, researching, synthesizing, taking inventory

- **Working with people**—administering, caring, confronting, counseling, demonstrating, mediating
- **Leadership**—arranging, competing, deciding, delegating, directing, explaining, influencing, initiating, managing, motivating, negotiating, planning, running, solving
- **Creative/Artistic**—creating, moving/dancing, drawing, expressing, performing, acting, presenting, designing, composing

In my case, the moves from journalism to public relations and then to freelance business communications required no special retraining because of the transferable skills common to all three—interviewing, researching, writing, editing, typing, word processing, and so on. Career experts break down such areas into even finer sets, such as the use of logic, analyzing, comprehending, interpreting, verbalizing, influencing, and forming conclusions. Rick Crow of the Cuyahoga County Reemployment Services Center tells counselees that most people have no idea how many skills they have. If you include learned behaviors all the way down to tying your shoes, experts have counted somewhere around 10,000 average "skills," he says.

In *When You Lose Your Job*, Cliff Hakim advocates taking stock of things in terms of a "career theme," which he defines as

> words, phrases, and feelings that have repeated throughout your career. For example, "helping others," "developing new ideas," or "making better what someone else has started." Think of it as a melody you've played—in the jobs you've had, in the projects you've completed, and in the roles you've assumed, both professionally and personally.[1]

Take a few minutes and make a personal inventory of your skills. Then keep the list as a future reference for considering how they may transfer to other employment, even a different career.

BIG BROTHER TO THE RESCUE

By the end of the first half of 2009, this Great Recession turned out to be the longest and most severe downturn with the greatest unemployment since the Great Depression, easily surpassing other recessions in recent decades. The President's Council of Economic Advisers projected that over the next five to ten years the long-term decline in the manufacturing sector should "moderate," construction industries could experience a modest recovery, and some other sectors—notably health care and "green" technologies, such as solar energy and bio-fuels—should continue strong growth. By the fourth quarter of 2010, the Council projected creation ("or retention") of an additional 3.5 million jobs as a result of the 2009 federal stimulus legislation (American Recovery and Reinvestment Act).[2] Only time, of course, will tell how much of that proves to be economic reality.

The U.S. Bureau of Labor Statistics (BLS) produces an *Occupational Outlook Handbook* and *Career Guide to Industries*, updated every two years. This is the authoritative reference for occupations according to training and education needed, earnings expected, job prospects, what workers do on the job, and working conditions. Other key features are rankings of occupations as hottest and coldest for prospective employees. Here, for example, are the ten occupations with the largest projected job declines through 2016—fields you definitely want to try to avoid or move out of:

1. Stock clerks and order fillers
2. Cashiers (except gaming)
3. Packers and packagers
4. File clerks
5. Farmers and ranchers
6. Order clerks
7. Sewing machine operators

8. Electrical and electronic equipment assemblers
9. Cutting, punching, and press machine setters, operators, and tenders, metal and plastic
10. Telemarketers

On the positive side, the BLS listed as the fastest-growing occupations:

1. Network systems and data communications analysts
2. Personal and home care aides
3. Home health aides
4. Computer software engineers, applications
5. Veterinary technologists and technicians
6. Personal financial advisers
7. Makeup artists, theatrical and performance
8. Medical assistants
9. Veterinarians
10. Substance abuse and behavioral disorder counselors

As a rate rather than an absolute number, "fastest-growing" does not necessarily translate into the greatest number of job opportunities. For that, here are the top ten occupations projected with the *largest* job growth:

1. Registered nurse
2. Retail salespersons
3. Customer service representatives
4. Combined food preparation and serving workers, including fast food
5. Office clerks, general
6. Personal and home care aides
7. Home health aides
8. Postsecondary teachers

9. Janitors and cleaners, except maids and housekeeping cleaners
10. Nursing aides, orderlies, and attendants

Here's a best-of-both-worlds slice of the data—the six best occupations in terms of fastest-growing *and* largest growth: Computer software engineers, application; computer systems analysts; network systems and data communications analysts; home health aides; medical assistants; personal and home care aides. Once available only in hard copy from public libraries or by special order from the Government Printing Office, the Handbook is now easily accessible online.[3]

GETTING THE DATA

Each of us as a whole person, of course, is much more than our isolated skill sets. Some job counselors advocate self-discovery in terms of our style (temperament and personality), skills (education and training), interests, and values. This can be tricky. Some Boomers raised during the Sputnik era, for example, may have difficulty appreciating their own aptitudes for liberal arts and "soft" science in light of their conditioning to place a much higher value on hard sciences, engineering, and technology. How many times have we heard of people who were highly successful in a good profession for which they had strong aptitude and skills but were totally miserable because it had lost its luster and become a joyless chore? Thousands of doctors, lawyers, accountants, and teachers have changed careers and repurposed themselves for this reason alone.

William Bridges (*JobShift*) recommends a DATA search—identifying your Desires, Abilities, Temperaments, and Assets. He couches Abilities in the form of the question, "What are you really good at?" These are the skills and talents—personal core competencies—that we have been considering. In their purest sense, these are our more general aptitudes—like mechanical or musical gifts—as opposed to the more developed proficiencies we normally think of as specific skills, such as drywall hanging or piano tuning.[4]

Temperament refers to our individual preferences and values that define our working and learning style, in which one environment is acceptable while another would be unsuitable or even frustrating. Such temperaments may be expressed in terms of a continuum, such as independence versus conformity, as measured by instruments like the Career Orientation Placement and Evaluation Survey (COPES)™. An independent type, for example, might work better as a freelancer than would a conformist, who is by nature more of a team player under supervision.

Other such work values include investigative vs. accepting; practical vs. carefree; leadership vs. supportive; orderliness vs. noncompulsive; recognition vs. privacy; aesthetic vs. realistic; social vs. self-concern. "Investigative," for example, describes the person who is intellectually curious and thrives on solving complex tasks. Other widely used systems include the Myers-Briggs Type Inventory (MBTI), which assesses temperaments according to sixteen types, and the Self-Directed Search (SDS), which helps match interests and abilities with specified career fields. Inventories like the COPES, MBTI, and SDS are useful tools for self-evaluation, although they require some interpretation and may be accessed through career counselors, who are generally listed in telephone directories under Career and Vocational Counselors.

By taking the COPES at the Cuyahoga County Reemployment Services Center, I verified that my work as a freelance writer was not just a situation by default, but was in line with my work values—my three highest being Investigative (intellectual curiosity), Aesthetic (artistic appreciation), and Independence. This was further confirmed by two other inventories, called the Career Ability Placement Survey (CAPS), and the Career Occupational Preference System (COPS-P), which showed both ability and interest in the areas of written and oral communications.

Job seekers taking the CAPS test are measured in eight primary areas—mechanical reasoning, spatial relations, verbal reasoning, numerical ability, language usage, word knowledge, perceptual speed and accuracy, and manual speed and dexterity. Those, of course, relate back to Abilities. These are different from our last "A" in DATA, Assets.

Assets are the relative advantages we may enjoy over others, all other things being equal, such as innate gifts and abilities. Although an ability or even one's temperament may be an asset, we are speaking primarily of the competitive advantages that come from experience. It may be having studied French or Spanish. It may be a network of contacts of people who can help by providing information or opening doors that are shut to others.

That leaves the area of interests—or the first letter in DATA, "D" for Desires. In terms of careers, the COPS-P groups them in eight major clusters: Science—medical/life and physical. Technology—electrical, mechanical, civil. Outdoor—nature and agribusiness. Business—finance and management. Computation. Communication—written and oral. Arts—performing and design. Service—instructional and social. For further information, you may want to consult the *Dictionary of Occupational Titles*. There is not much ground left uncovered by this system. Someone bitten by the bug to become a ski instructor, for example, may be surprised to find himself listed under "Arts, Entertaining-Performing" DOT #153.227-018.

We are not referring here, however, to career decisions driven so much by things such as pay or benefits or status, but by, as some have put it, what makes our "toes tingle." It may be a radical idea to some, but it's about what we enjoy doing, the things that bring us personal fulfillment in their performance. Bridges suggests that some of the questions we may want to ask ourselves to identify these desires include: What do I want (open-ended)? What do I want to be doing and how do I want to be living in ten years? What was I meant to accomplish with my life? [5]

"CHARACTER" SKILLS

There are other skills that we seldom think of because they're almost too familiar; we use them every day to survive and make life work. They are called "adaptive skills" because they allow us to adapt or adjust to a variety of situations, including work. They could also be called "good worker traits" because they are especially valued by employers, such as getting to work on time and getting along well with others.

Other adaptive skills:

- **Quality**—productive, assertive, capable, competent, creative, efficient, independent, intelligent, original, persistent, resourceful, practical, strong, tenacious, versatile, well-organized
- **Attitude**—cheerful, accepts supervision, flexible, energetic, eager, enthusiastic, motivated, friendly, good-natured, modest, optimistic, confident
- **Work ethic**—honest, dependable, reliable, discreet, good attendance, conscientious, helpful, loyal, patient, responsible, sincere, steady, thrifty, trustworthy

Here are some of the leadership-related qualities from my researcher friend Steve Kipp, who culled them from several sources (including a leadership book by George Barna[6] and *The Leadership Bible* [7]):

- **General qualities**—loving, joyful, peaceful, patient, kind, good, faithful, gentle, self-controlled, temperate, respectable, hospitable, able to teach, not quarrelsome, not a lover of money or pursuing dishonest gain, not given to drunkenness, good family and household manager, good reputation, sincere, tested, passion for spiritual goodness, morally pure, culturally sensitive

- **Leadership character traits**—servant's heart, honest, loyal, trustworthy, courageous, risk-taker, humble, sensitive, teachable, values-driven, optimistic, even-tempered, gentle, consistent, spiritually deep, forgiving, compassionate, energetic, self-controlled, wise, discerning, encouraging, passionate, fair, merciful, reliable
- **Specific competencies**—long-range planning; initiating strategic action; dealing with change; system process thinking; resource development; commitment to quality and excellence; servant leadership; influence and persuasion; integrity, values, and character; empowerment, delegation, authority, and responsibility; stress management; casting vision; creating a viable corporate culture; team building; coaching, mentoring, developing, and managing people; conflict management and resolution; stewardship and time management; effective communication

Conversely, there are traits and behaviors that are about as endearing to employers as higher taxes. Absenteeism and tardiness naturally rank high on employer surveys as major reasons for firing an employee. But even higher are negative personal characteristics, including lying, dishonesty, ego problems, arrogance, overconfidence, aggressiveness, lack of dedication or commitment, unconcern, not being a team player, poor attitude, and being a poor listener.

Other characteristics that rub employers wrong include not getting along, poor communicating, whining, complaining, poor attitude toward the company, not utilizing one's full potential, laziness, lack of motivation or enthusiasm. Even poor eye contact, excessive nervousness, lack of creativity, and lack of integrity make the problem list. Poor work habits leading to discharge include not following instructions, not doing the job, lack of productivity, not finishing tasks, "goofing off" and "fooling around," doing personal business on company time, irresponsibility,

unreliability, unpredictability, inconsisten-
cies, not following policy or procedures,
poor decisions, and incompetence.

How important is
character? It may
determine our
very destiny.

It should be apparent by now that the
so-called adaptive skills—or lack thereof—
add up to much the same thing as character
qualities. And how important is character? It may
determine our very destiny. Consider the following old
saying: "Sow a thought, reap an action. Sow an action, reap a
habit. Sow a habit, reap a character. Sow a character, reap a des-
tiny." Or as the German poet Novalis (Friedrich von Harden-
berg) put it more succinctly: "Character is destiny." On this, too,
King Solomon had words of wisdom: "For as he thinketh in his
heart, so is he" (Proverbs 23:7 KJV).

Character is the missing dimension of virtues in the equa-
tion of talents, skills, gifts, desires, abilities, temperament, and
assets. It is the work ethic and the moral quality of our lives that
will endure after we are gone. On the way to our destiny, it is the
difference we make in life—and the lives of others.

The story is told of a carpenter who was given the task of
building an entire house unsupervised with only a specified
budget and a reasonable deadline. The man, thinking himself
clever, built the house with a minimum of effort, cutting corners
on quality wherever he could, disregarding even safety consider-
ations. He finished so far ahead of schedule that he spent the next
few workdays fishing. When he returned to work, the owner of
the construction company surprised him with a set of keys: The
house that he had been building so haphazardly was a gift—for
him. The carpenter, considering the miserable heap he had cre-
ated, realized too late that he had no one to blame but himself.

Some people who have studied character extensively have
come up with some intriguing findings. One of those is the fact
that character qualities, like vocational skills, tend to appear in
clusters. Again, like other abilities, these qualities can be developed

and strengthened through consistent discipline. And these clusters can be used to define entire character types, which relates directly to our journey of self-discovery.

Two different organizations have teamed up in this pioneering area: Kimray, Inc., a manufacturer of oil and gas equipment and controls, serving producers and equipment manufacturers in the petroleum industry, and the Institute of Basic Life Principles (IBLP), headed by Bill Gothard, an evangelical Christian well known for his teaching ministry in huge urban seminars. Tom Hill, Kimray chief operating officer, saw what he thought was great potential business application in IBLP's teachings on character qualities, and the two organizations together spawned a new venture called the Character Training Institute in a former Holiday Inn hotel in Oklahoma City, a few blocks from the bombed-out federal building.

"The more rules you make, the more rules you need," Hill said at one of the Institute's first three-day training programs for businesspeople. "You can't write enough rules." He was teaching the businesspeople that good character is an inward motivation springing from the heart that needs to be cultivated by good managers through praise and recognition. His remarks carried the weight of credibility as he explained what cultivating character had done for his business—including reduced employee absenteeism and improved net income.

In the Character First training program, managers learn to identify forty-nine discrete character qualities in employees in seven clusters of seven—such as self-control, respectfulness, diligence, thoroughness, dependability, security, and patience. That particular cluster defines the character type known as the Teacher, with which I instantly identified. The teacher is defined as one who "imparts wisdom, maturity, and skill to others, validates direction, and ensures completion."

The point is that these principles are not just for managers. They may be helpful signposts along the self-discovery journey for the displaced worker and job seeker, anyone who needs to reinvent his career. Negative personal traits can be diamonds in the rough. If you struggle with being rigid, harsh, overbearing, judgmental, and miserly, cheer up; you may have the character quality of self-control in a distorted measure. Character First sorts through the qualities and their distortions.

The other character types are:

- **Visionary**—sees beyond the immediate situation.
- **Server**—meets the needs of others to help them succeed.
- **Organizer**—directs resources for successful completion of goals.
- **Mediator**—compassionately analyzes merits of competing positions.
- **Idealist**—identifies problems, speaks the truth boldly.
- **Provider**—ensures the best use of available resources.

Everyone has character, positive or negative. What type are you? For further information go to www.characterfirst.com.

7

OVERCOMING
REJECTION

NOTE: *This story may be fictional, but it's no less real. In a sense, it happens all the time.*

The phone rang, but Jerry knew Beth would get it. He was taking a nap on the couch, and there was no particular reason to get up just yet. It wasn't quite nine o'clock, and he still felt under the weather from the lingering effects of this most recent cold. He seemed to get a lot of those these days. He turned over and tried to get back to sleep.

Jerry Davenport had become a real couch potato. In the six months since he had lost his job, he had gained twenty pounds just from inactivity. But he felt he deserved to take it easy after years of beating his brains out in those sweatshops where he used to work until getting cast aside like a piece of refuse.

"Jerry!" called Beth. "Get up! It's the woman from the Displaced Worker Center. She wants to know if you can come in at ten."

Jerry raised his drowsy head in irritation. "Ten? That's only an hour. Ask her if I can see her tomorrow."

Beth gave a little snort of apparent frustration and returned to the kitchen. Jerry could still hear her from the living room.

"Yes, Ms. Tompkins," she said emphatically. "Jerry will be there at ten. Thank you very much."

Uh-oh. Jerry sensed an incident in the making. This suspicion was instantly confirmed as the floorboards telegraphed Beth's determined stride coming through the dining room.

"Jerry!" she barked. "If you don't get up off that couch and act like you're alive, I'm going to give you a cold shower with a bucket."

"Go 'way," Jerry murmured.

Beth was insistent. "I am not going away. And you're getting up off that couch and going downtown to that appointment or I'll—"

Jerry propped himself up on one elbow and gave her a challenging look. "Or you'll what?"

Beth was biting her lip. "Or I'm leaving you, Jerry. And I mean it!"

With that, she spun on her heel and left the room as quickly as she'd entered. Jerry was nonplussed. This wasn't like Beth. Normally she didn't make threats like that. Somehow, Jerry believed she wasn't kidding.

"Nice to meet you, Mr. Davenport," said Juanita Tompkins, the job counselor. "Let's just take a minute and fill out this questionnaire. First, why don't you give me your employment history."

Jerry shrugged. "What do you want to know?"

"The basics—the places you worked, how long, what you did there, what skills were required, what you liked about it."

Jerry took a deep breath and thought back twenty-five years. He was first a stereotyper in the composing room at the *Daily Slant*, turning out page plates for the press room in the old hot-lead process. He did that for nearly ten years until the newspaper announced that it was converting to a cold-type process that would eliminate stereotyping—and stereotypers. During the transition Jerry took some training and did some apprenticing through the union as a keyliner, but his seniority was not high enough to land a permanent slot when the dust cleared.

So for the next several years he tried a variety of low-paying jobs until he could find something in his field. He worked as a convenience store clerk, painted houses, and served as assistant manager of a video rental store until he landed a full-time position as a keyliner, pasting up pages with a razor knife and wax gun for a magazine published locally for car collectors. There he received valuable on-the-job-training in photographic film processing. Unfortunately, three years into that job the magazine was sold to a larger publisher, who moved the jobs of Jerry and others in his department to Baltimore.

It was back to painting houses for another year until he got a good job as a photographic processor for a large store in town. His previous experience qualified him for a supervisor's position and better pay than the processing machine operators he supervised. Unfortunately, that higher pay made him a target when things went south and set him up for the next layoff. The last two years he worked there the business was steadily declining, reportedly a victim of the boom in digital photography that allowed consumers to print their own photos or use only the electronic images. Unknowingly, Jerry had been training his replacement, who was willing to work for lower pay and kept his job when half the department was let go months ago—including Jerry.

"And how old are you, Mr. Davenport?" asked Ms. Tompkins when he'd finished his account.

"Fifty-two," he said. "Please call me Jerry."

She looked up with a sympathetic expression. "Sure, Jerry. So, were you laid off or let go?"

Jerry lowered his eyes. "Let go. Nobody's getting called back."

"How does that make you feel?"

He looked up in mild surprise. "What? You want to know how I . . . feel?"

The woman nodded.

Jerry wasn't sure what to say. "Well, I don't know. I'm OK, I guess."

The woman looked skeptical. "I'm serious. You have feelings, don't you?"

Jerry stiffened. "Yeah, sure. But what's the use? It won't change anything. You just take your lumps and move on."

"Do you?"

Something in the way she said it irritated him. "That's right. What do you mean?"

"Well, you've been out of work almost six months, and still no job. And your wife says you're a basketcase—'no oomph,' I think she said."

Now Jerry was really annoyed. "She said that?"

Ms. Tompkins nodded. "Is it true?"

He was beginning to get the picture. "Well, maybe it's not so easy anymore finding a job. Don't you think it's normal to get a little discouraged?"

The woman nodded again. "It's also normal for a spouse to feel frustrated. So, you feel discouraged—'a little.' What's that like?"

Jerry shrugged. "No big deal. It just takes me a little longer to get rolling these days, that's all."

"Why do you think that is?"

"Well, I'm over fifty now. Doesn't that mean I should be over the hill or something?"

Ms. Tompkins ignored his feeble attempt at humor. "OK.

Being older makes it harder to find a job. That doesn't make you angry?"

Now Jerry was starting to get a little stubborn. "Don't think so. Should it?"

"Maybe. Maybe you are and you don't know it. Maybe there's some guilt there, too."

Jerry almost laughed. "What are you, a shrink or something?"

The woman smiled. "I'm a licensed psychologist and counselor. How is everything at home?"

Jerry felt defensive. "You mean, like with the wife and kids?"

She nodded.

"OK, I guess."

The woman looked skeptical again. "No conflict?"

He caught himself. "Well, I take that back. My wife threatened to leave me if I didn't get it together. I don't know why she's acting like that."

"How does that make you feel?"

"I think she's being unreasonable, that's all. Maybe I just don't get it."

The woman smiled kindly. "Look. I'm not really trying to do a whole counseling session here, but I am trying to show you that you need to open up. I think your wife is trying to get you to do that, too. You're shut down, Jerry. You need to deal with it, not stuff it."

It was Jerry's turn to be skeptical. He had the improbable mental image of a boarded-up gas station. "I'm shut down?"

She nodded. "Think about it. Shouldn't you be upset—concerned, at least—that your wife would consider leaving you?"

"I don't know. Maybe. I guess I don't like thinking about it. The last thing I need is . . . something else to worry about."

The woman paused. "Do you love your wife?"

Suddenly, feelings started welling up—like what it would be like to lose Beth. There were definitely things worse than losing your job, he realized.

"Yes," he barely managed to croak. There seemed to be something in his throat. Maybe this woman knew what she was talking about.

"Does she know it?"

Jerry flared a bit. "Yes, she does," he insisted with a hint of indignation.

Ms. Tompkins smiled again. "Well, you're probably not alexithymic."

"Alexi—what?"

"Alexithymic. It means being unable to express feelings—literally, 'no words for emotions.' We sometimes call it flat affect. With people who are out of work, it's usually a temporary condition, but it can be incapacitating until you deal with those feelings and work through them."

Jerry nodded. "So, what's happening to me is normal, as a result of losing my job?"

"Look at it this way," the woman suggested. "Did you lose your job—or did your job lose you?"

For the first time that day, Jerry smiled. Maybe for the first time in days.

The next day was Jerry's first full day at the center. The morning was spent learning his way around the facility, meeting the instructor, and accessing the computer database. The afternoon was spent in a classroom with some instruction and small group breakouts.

Jerry wasn't sure whether the morning or the afternoon was the more enlightening. He found that the computer lab was a place he might spend some time learning some new skills. He used the interactive workstation with a touch-screen allowing him to access a wide variety of related subjects. Since Juanita Tompkins had piqued his curiosity about the trick bag of repressed emotions, this was the subject area he chose to pursue. The process reminded him of the bank phone lines or voice-mail systems that prompt callers to select numbered options in a decision tree.

He chose to track subjects related to unemployment, stress, and family problems and was surprised by some of the things he found:

- Jerry was not alone. Each month thousands of middle-aged American men were losing their jobs at a time when their personal and family responsibilities were the greatest. Middle-aged men had become the most inviting targets because of their higher pay.
- Closely related to job loss was a high incidence of depression, panic attacks, and drug and alcohol abuse. Emergency rooms and mental health facilities were reporting a measurable increase in job-related emotional distress that in most severe forms can lead to suicide.
- Studies showed a correlation between unemployment and increases in anger, intense marital conflict, inconsistent parenting, and even child abuse and neglect. And children themselves suffered from self-blame, lowered self-esteem, confusion, insecurity, worry, withdrawal, depression, anger, and irritability, which often resulted in increased misbehavior.

Jerry thought about how it seemed that Beth and their two teenagers, Jason and Nicki, had been picking on him. They even accused him of being mean and ill-tempered. It hadn't made sense. Why was he being so misunderstood? He knew he'd probably been a little grouchy at first. Maybe now he was being perceived that way all the time, rightly or wrongly. It was worth a thought.

In the afternoon their instructor, Howard Somerville, told Jerry and the dozen other participants that they still had jobs: "Your job right now is finding another job." Howard introduced them to the reference works available to job seekers, explaining that there were more than twelve thousand different job classifications.

Jerry flipped through some of these thick references, the *Dictionary of Occupational Titles,* the *Guide for Occupational Exploration,* and the *Occupational Outlook Handbook.* They were the size of big-city telephone books. If there were that many other fields, he thought, maybe he could find something by changing his career path. Maybe Howard or somebody else at this place could explain how that could be done.

"The way of finding a job these days has changed," Howard told the group. "It used to be that you could find most of the available jobs by checking the classified ads, job postings, and company human resource departments. Not so anymore. Those only account for one-fourth of the available jobs today. So, if you're just applying for the jobs you see in the Sunday paper, you're missing about three-fourths of them. That three-fourths is what we call the 'hidden job market.' That takes some directed strategies to reach, such as networking, that we are going to discuss."

The average person has accumulated from five hundred to a thousand personal contacts.

Networking means taking stock of your circle of friends and associates—which is probably a lot larger than you think, he told them. And when you count their friends and associates, it can add up to countless potential opportunities. Howard challenged the group to swallow their pride and alert the people in their networks to their plight. Chances are, he said, someone out there knows about a golden employment opportunity—and someone you should talk to about it. Most people are more than happy to help, especially as the downsizing/layoff problem has become commonplace.

The average person has accumulated from five hundred to a thousand personal contacts, he said. That means each connection between two individuals yields between 250,000 (500 times 500) and a million (1,000 times 1,000) potential contacts. He illustrated the power of the network with an experiment by social psychologist Stanley Milgram, who asked randomly selected people in Kansas and Nebraska to try to reach specific unknown individuals in Massachusetts through their networks. While observers guessed it might take a hundred such contacts to reach the intended destination, the average in Milgram's experiment was five and a half—and as few as two.[1]

This factor has become popularly known as "degrees of separation." It has taken wing most recently in the form of Internet social networking—sites like Facebook, MySpace, Twitter, and Linkedin—that have made exploiting this dynamic easier—and more effective—than ever before.

The moral of the story, Howard said, is that when it comes to finding a job, it's both what you know and who you know—or who someone you know knows. For many people, the network has proven to be the single most reliable way of finding the next opportunity. Don't delay listing your contacts and making those phone calls, he said. And don't make the mistake of failing to give feedback to the person who helped you, he added. Let the person know and convey your thanks. It will make that person feel good about continuing to help you.

Then he threw the subject out for discussion. "Why do you suppose the vast majority of job opportunities are hidden?"

A talkative older man at another table raised his hand. "I don't know what they do with the good jobs, but those aren't the ones they advertise. I can tell you that from personal experience. I think the whole reason they have to advertise them in the first place is they can't find anybody with those qualifications or there's something wrong with the job, like the pay or the working conditions or the company itself."

Howard nodded. "Yeah. Want ads have been good for some specific fields like information technology and health care, but otherwise there's often a reason they have to advertise those jobs.

Increasingly, the good jobs are filled by word-of-mouth through personal contacts, often through other employees. If you're an employee, managers know you're only going to recommend somebody who's really good because your credibility is on the line too. Also, word-of-mouth is faster and cheaper. That means as a job-seeker you have to do the same thing yourself that the employers are doing—network. You have to learn the art of self-marketing."

Jerry wasn't terribly surprised. He'd been doing the Sunday classified-ad routine for months, and he'd had a feeling he was missing the boat. But in his bummed-out frame of mind, he kind of didn't care half the time. Maybe that wasn't such a good attitude. He knew a lot of people were regularly surfing the job-posting websites. He'd even been on Monster.com once and realized it wasn't so mysterious after all. He made a mental note to start doing more of that on a regular basis.

Howard asked them to look at their information sheets. They showed the fastest-growing and fastest-declining occupations, as projected by the U.S. Bureau of Labor Statistics through the year 2016. Several titles jumped out at him. Not too far down the page of fastest-declining occupations, almost as high as "telemarketers," was his old trade, "photographic processing machine operators." That didn't surprise him. It hadn't been virtually legislated out of existence, like telemarketing, but it was just as clearly becoming a dead end.

Maybe he should go over that list of fastest-growing jobs and get into another line of work, Jerry thought, although it made him feel somehow a little disloyal to his old trade, which was probably a bit silly. That was like feeling sentimental about yesterday's newspaper instead of turning a new page on today's. He thought he'd also heard talk that there was now money available for the kind of re-training he'd be looking for to make that kind of change. It was something; at least, he'd have to check out.

Just then, someone began ringing a bell out in the hall. Jerry wondered at first if it was a fire alarm, but it sounded more like a hand bell, like the old-fashioned brass kind they used to have in the public schools.

"What's that?" said the older man sitting across the table from Jerry. Others were looking around, too.

Howard was smiling. "One of our graduates just got a job. Has anyone seen the movie *It's a Wonderful Life*, with Jimmy Stewart?"

A number of hands went up.

"In the movie they'd ring a bell in heaven whenever an angel got his wings. Here, we ring the bell whenever someone gets a job. You'll get used to hearing that around here."

Jerry realized he was smiling again. That made twice in two days.

That afternoon the twelve participants were asked to break up into three subgroups and discuss case studies of several people who had been thrown out of work with slim prospects of getting rehired, largely because of age and outdated skills. Jerry was most appalled by the insensitive treatment these people had received from their former employers. A fifty-five-year-old woman figuratively received her pink slip in remote fashion along with several other coworkers over the public address system in their work room. A forty-five-year-old man was asked to clean out his desk with a supervisor looking on and then was escorted out the front door by a security officer.

Howard had asked them to come up with some of the feelings these people must have had, and the words poured forth. *Betrayal. Fear. Worthlessness. Self-hate. Pity. Withdrawal. Helplessness. Desperation. Anxiety. Shame.*

"Anger!" Jerry called out emphatically.

There was an awkward moment of silence as heads turned his way. Jerry swallowed hard. Maybe he'd said it a little loudly. He was surprised to find himself feeling a little warm around the collar. He wasn't just imagining the anger of these other people; he was feeling some of his own ire.

"Well," he added, lowering his voice. "These people were treated like they were less than human, like they had done something wrong—or like criminals, even."

A woman about his age named Jasmine nodded. "Like dogs."

An older man named George frowned. "I came back from vacation and found my desk had been cleaned out. Nobody knew what had become of my stuff. They just told me I didn't work there anymore."

A younger fellow named Jeff smiled, but his voice sounded almost menacing. "Makes you understand what happens with some of those postal workers."

Jerry found himself agreeing, but he was startled by his own bitterness. What was happening to him? Was he going off the deep end? Surely he would never approve of violence. But he could understand what Jeff was getting at. Did that make him a bad guy? Jerry was confused. He wasn't sure how he was supposed to feel, but it wasn't as if he had that much control over it.

When Howard ended the discussion, he suggested that some of them may have been able to relate to the stories they'd discussed. He hoped that some of them might even be able to discuss their own feelings.

"How many of you find it easy to talk to your friends and family about these things?" he asked.

There were no hands.

"Why not?" Howard asked.

Maybe he was angrier than he realized or allowed himself to feel.

"They don't understand," said a man named Cody. "They haven't been through it. They just say, 'Don't worry. Everything will be OK.' Or worse, 'Why don't you just go out and find a job?'"

Howard nodded. "That seems to be what happens. It's called 'minimizing.' With all good intentions, people tend to encourage us to bottle up our feelings when we really need to work them out. Somehow they may think that's being helpful. But how do you feel as a result?"

"Isolated!" someone called out.

"That's right," Howard continued. "But I think some of you found it was easier to open up with strangers here in your small groups because they understand what you're going through."

Jerry remembered how he'd felt when he said the word *anger* and recalled Juanita Tompkins's words the day before. Maybe he was angrier than he realized or allowed himself to feel.

Now Howard was writing on the whiteboard. "Rejection. Job loss is all about rejection. Here's one model for understanding your relational style, especially in terms of how you deal with feelings of rejection. Some of it's taken from a book called *Neanderthals at Work*, and some of it is taken from a Christian counseling expert named Neil Anderson.

"You can be a Competitor or a Believer or a Rebel. The Competitor is a controller who handles things by trying to beat the system—whether it's school or work or society in general. He is self-sufficient, but he is unable to express his feelings and struggles with perfectionism and worry. The Believer tries to get life through the system and so is cut to the heart by rejection, alternating between anger and feelings of worthlessness and poor self-esteem, to say the least."

Jerry froze. He felt as if Howard were reading about him.

"Then there's the Rebel," Howard continued. "As his name says, the Rebel rebels against the system. He fights the fire of rejection with fire of his own. 'You can't fire me—I quit!' he would say, even if he cuts off his own nose and burns his own bridges, ending up without severance or unemployment benefits. The Rebel struggles with a great deal of bitterness toward others as well as self-hatred."

A younger Hispanic woman named Maria raised her hand with a question. "Can you be more than one type? I identify with all three of those."

"Absolutely," said Howard, smiling. "Most of us are predominantly one type, but we may move in and out of the others, depending on our circumstances and what seems to meet our needs at the moment."

Jerry leaned back heavily. There was a lot to think about, an awful lot. But at least there was some assurance in knowing that others had been there before and there were ways of dealing with these sorts of things. Maybe he didn't have to be a victim of his own reactions, with the world pushing his preprogrammed buttons. It even helped knowing that there were others worse off than himself. *At least*, he thought, *I know I'm not alone.*

8

SURVIVAL
AND SELF-MARKETING

Over the next three days our fictional Jerry Davenport received a wealth of practical information about searching for a new job. For the first two days he learned about survival skills and goal setting and how to write a personal mission statement, a résumé, a Minute Pitch, and an action plan. On the third day he came to grips with a new direction for his life by reinventing his career.

   The following is an account of those three days.

SURVIVAL SKILLS

Think of a career like a car, Howard told Jerry's group. Being out of a job is like driving on a curve. If you don't slow down, there's going to be trouble. Same thing with your lifestyle. If you try to keep up the same standard of living after losing your job, you're going to put too much pressure on yourself and possibly wipe out financially. Unemployment compensation is not great income. It's not supposed to be. It's only supposed to be a temporary safety net for survival. And bankruptcy is no fun. You need to reduce your expenditures quickly.

The higher the lost income, the longer it may take to replace. One rule of thumb is an average of one month for every $10,000 of lost pay. So, you could expect to take about four months to find a comparable job if you're a typical blue-collar worker, maybe six or seven months for higher-paid professionals, and even a year or more for high-level business executives. Knowing that, you shouldn't get frustrated and discouraged if you don't land a job the first couple of weeks. But neither should you become complacent, especially if you see too much time passing by.

In addition to rejection/dejection, you and your family may suffer from a sense of deprivation. It may seem unfair, but you are going to have less wherewithal in your time of greatest need. It's all a matter of perspective. In pioneer days, people worked long enough to meet their basic needs for food, clothing, and shelter, and then they did other things, like rest or recreate. Subsistence meant working until you had enough, then stopping. But since the Industrial Revolution and the factory-model workplace, our work lives have become prepackaged increments of time and pay, creating mass-produced expectations of houses, cars, wardrobes, gadgets, and other consumables. Then there's Madison Avenue's "market-induced demand," which gets us desiring things we don't even need. Then when we have to give things up, we feel deprived in comparison to what we've grown used to and what the rest of our world considers the norm.

But is the norm "normal"? "Enough" has become something entirely different from what it once was. We are now locked into an artificial standard of living of high expectations—the American ideal of affluence, creature comfort, and instant gratification—that leaves frustration in its absence. We may not be able to turn the clock back to an earlier century, but we can reduce our cost of living and downscale, conserve, and economize—i.e., slow down before we wipe out on the curve.

Freedom is not being trapped by a personal debt load exceeding annual income by nearly one-third, as is the average U.S. family, according to the Federal Reserve Bank. This includes mortgages, credit cards, auto and other consumer loans. When much of that is on credit cards, it can become an enslavement because we may become unable to pay any more than the minimum monthly charge and no longer be able to reduce the principal. Even with a regular income, that's a problem. When that person becomes unemployed, it can be financially disastrous, often leading to bankruptcy. Howard gave the group some handouts consisting of a family budget worksheet, a list of household expenses that could be cut or reduced, and samples of suggested letters that can be sent to creditors proposing a deferred payment schedule.

"Use common sense," Howard told the group. "You're not the first ones to be laid off." Businesspeople are well aware of the downsizing/layoff phenomenon. In the business world, vendors are used to waiting ninety days for payment from customers. Many times creditors can be persuaded to accept deferred payment, especially if they sense you are sincere. And this is certainly more honorable than defaulting on the debt entirely.

Meanwhile, you can control the damage from this point on and stop the bleeding by reducing expenses. Put away your credit cards. Cut them up and throw them away if they control you instead of vice versa. It may be easier said than done, but you can eliminate everything but the necessities—heat, food, shelter, health care, and so on. Necessities do not include cable TV, carry-out pizza, magazine subscriptions, athletic club memberships, and new clothes. But it might include a new business outfit if that's what it takes to get a new job.

This is the time to get serious. You may question having cable service shut off if you think you might get a job in a few weeks, but these days the average wait is much longer than that. By the time you're proved wrong, it's too late. You may be able to return a sweater you shouldn't have bought, but you can't unwatch three months of cable TV or uneat a bunch of carryout meals. It may also seem like such small economies that you question what difference they could make. But taken together as a whole, they can be quite significant. You are going to have a hard enough time paying the old bills accumulated prior to your discharge, let alone incurring new expenses.

Miscellaneous:

- *Don't burn your bridges.* Resist the impulse to bad-mouth your former employer to his face or behind his back. You may be able to obtain a helpful letter of reference if your discharge was not your fault and you left on amicable terms. This can give you tremendous credibility with any prospective employer who might otherwise be concerned about hiring a potential problem person. Employers will understand that you were just an ordinary casualty, like thousands of others.
- *Treat looking for work like a job.* Think of it as an assignment and avoid the "hundred-pound telephone" and "twenty-pound tongue" problem that plagues job-seekers. Don't succumb to the "night owl" temptation. Get out of bed in the morning and keep regular business hours. While few people can stomach working the telephone or pounding the pavement for eight-hour stretches, a significant portion of the workweek should be devoted to the

work search. You might want to reserve one day of the week for a different project—like finally painting the house, doing your genealogy, or attending your child's choir concert—and using the other four for job-hunting. Part-time volunteerism, especially if it puts you in contact with those less fortunate than yourself, can be a wonderful tonic. Mondays, which are often the most discouraging day for jobless people, are great for this sort of thing.

To cultivate a success mind-set, establish some reasonable secondary goals.

- *Identify your top professional and personal goals* and write them down on a time line—i.e., three months, six months, a year. Your primary goal is to find employment, but that should not be your *only* goal. Otherwise, your daily mind-set until you reach that goal may be failure. To cultivate a success mind-set, establish some reasonable secondary goals. Losing forty or fifty pounds might be admirable, but the likelihood of failure may only raise your stress level or compound your woes. Just establishing an exercise regimen, no matter how modest, may be more realistic. Goal areas to consider include family, friends, associates, income, savings, investments, purchases, fitness, health, appearance, nutrition, recreation, relaxation, training, education, travel, and hobbies. Spend some time nurturing your relationship with your spouse, which might be under considerable stress. Christians, of course, can use this time as a great opportunity to get deeper into the Word and closer to God. If you do these things right, the period of unemployment need not be "lost" time.

Some of these principles are foundational. Once you have identified both short- and long-range goals, you can begin constructing a specific action plan employing your personal values, skills, and interests. For example, if you identify a new vocational field to pursue, you might find you need to acquire some additional skills, which means your action plan should include a strategy for obtaining some further education or training.

The Christian perspective, however, necessarily takes us beyond mere self-preservation. There is a sense in which we consider ourselves even expendable. Laid-off researcher Steve Kipp vividly recalls a chapel message years ago by Azusa Pacific professor Les Blank, who described his reaction to the news he was going blind. He said he came to a fork in the road where he realized he either needed to consider himself "expendable" or to become "self-survival" oriented. He chose the former.

"In an economic/vocational crisis, our trigger response is going to be self-survival oriented," said Kipp. "But Jesus Christ and the apostle Paul are our examples of considering themselves expendable on behalf of others—and that even includes for us the idea of assisting others in finding work ahead of ourselves."

CREATING A RÉSUMÉ

Why should you write a personal mission statement? Because its content can be key to the other statements you will need to make in your employment search—from an action plan to a résumé to a short personal presentation. Even if no one else were ever to see this statement, just going through the thought process is worthwhile. Apart from simple honesty, there are no wrong answers. Think in terms of "the purpose for which I was put here on earth." Then you can get more specific in vocational terms.

Jerry turned in his first stab at a personal mission statement, and the next day Juanita helped him to phrase it better. Jerry Davenport's Mission Statement:

I enjoy producing high-quality publications and images with graphics and text that bring helpful information, entertainment, and amusement to large numbers of people. I work best as a team player in a large organization in a creative, nonsupervisory capacity. I am committed first and foremost to the welfare of my family and am considering new career directions as necessary, but prefer not to have night shifts or travel that would take me from my family.

Juanita said, yes, mission or purpose statements can and should change over time in detail as circumstances and your understanding change, but the primary thrust should endure. That's why she steered Jerry away from stating a specific field such as keyliner or photo processor. She looked at the doodlings in his notebook and asked if he had ever done anything in the art field. He told her he used to draw a lot for fun but had never pursued it seriously. Juanita suggested that he take some tests that might indicate whether something like graphic design might be a career option for him, since he was interested in the three main ingredients—publishing, computers, and design.

In class, Howard asked the group to take their mission statements and apply them to the creation of a résumé. Jerry had a résumé of sorts that was just a list of previous jobs. It definitely needed upgrading. The class learned how to craft an initial "Objective" statement at the top that is half job wanted, half mission statement of no more than two dozen words. An example of an Objective statement from an abstracter/indexer for business and technical publications: "A support position in a library or publishing center using my proven research, organizational, and training skills to contribute to effective information transfer."

This statement's strength is that it isn't "gimme, gimme"-oriented. It will appeal to employers because it emphasizes not so much what the applicant wants to get out of the company as what he or she would contribute to the work or the organization.

In that light, the Jerry Davenport résumé objective should state: "A position in the publishing field where I can be an effective team member in the production of high-quality publications with text and graphics." That is specific enough to get the point across, but general enough to keep his options open for a different division within the same occupational field—such as graphic design or electronic pagination systems, assuming he were to get the additional training.

As for the rest of the résumé, Jerry's old version was like the "chronological" résumé with his work history listed in reverse order from most recent to earliest. Besides an initial Objective, Howard suggested that Jerry add a Summary of Qualifications and a Related Experiences section. Qualifications—the first place many employers look—should describe several abilities and skills, such as the equipment he knows how to operate and the tasks he is trained to perform. The specific training or education itself would be listed elsewhere under its own separate section. Related Experiences could be optional or miscellaneous items, such as other accomplishments, awards, affiliations, organizations, workshops, associations, and relevant volunteer work.

A different version of the résumé is the "functional" format, which is organized according to skill or experience categories rather than time periods, Howard told the group. It can be useful when you have made career changes or there are gaps in your work history. The downside is that employers may think you are hiding something, such as a jail term. Yet another version, the "combination" format, takes the best of the chronological and functional formats. It is done either by adding an Experience section to the functional format to feature the work history or by emphasizing accomplishments within each unit of the chronological list. The combination format has become popular because of its versatility.

Whatever the format, your résumé needs to grab the potential employer's attention and be effortless to read. It is a self-marketing tool, potentially the most powerful one you have, and is a warm-up for the employment interview. Whereas an employment application tells the employer what he wants to know, the résumé lets the applicant turn the tables to choose the information he wants to present. Some companies now are storing scanned images of employment applications and résumés in their computer systems, referenced by key words or phrases related to the company's objectives. How to capitalize on that: If the company is advertising a position, check the ad for specific wording of the qualifications sought and adjust your résumé accordingly. With the right words, you might just show up on the right screen at the right time. When applying online: Create a second version of your résumé in text-only (.txt) format specifically for pasting into the application. This enhances the readability of your résumé by modern HR software. Avoid all formatting elements such as bullets (substitute asterisks) or boldface (capitalize for emphasis). And to avoid unwanted wrap lines, make sure no line is longer than fifty-six characters, using forced (hard) returns at the end of each line.

A good résumé may not directly land you a job, but it can help you survive at least the first cut.

Experts disagree on résumé length, Howard said. Some say employers don't want to see anything longer than one page, whereas others say not to try to cram everything onto one page. Probably safe advice is to condense where practical, especially where it helps readability. If it's not that much over a page, condense some more until it fits onto one page. Professional résumé services can help for a fee, but the results will only be as good as the information and direction you provide the service. They shouldn't be expected to get the right emphasis where you have been less than clear.

If you don't get professional help, at least have another pair of good eyes look at the résumé before it goes anywhere. Misspellings, bad grammar, typographical errors, sloppiness, and other errors will be held against you—fairly or not—as a reflection of your work ethic. On the other hand, a good résumé may not directly land you a job, but it can help you survive at least the first cut as the employer reduces his mountain of applications.

AIDA AND THE MINUTE PITCH

After fixing up their résumés, the group constructed their Minute Pitches. These are for situations where you have only a very short time to make your case to someone in the process of networking and making phone contacts and even in an actual job interview, Howard said. It is your core message and is sometimes called by other names, including the "Short Personal Presentation," the "Thirty-Second Commercial," and the "Ninety-Second Self-Presentation." Since it is a form of direct marketing appeal, it should adhere to the time-honored salesman's success formula, AIDA—attempting to arouse the listener's Attention, Interest, Desire, and Action. That means it should be more than just informational content for the intellect, but should appeal to the will and even emotions. The visceral level is where acceptance /rejection decisions about people are often made.

The savvy job prospector will apply the distinction between features and benefits to his own product—himself. The features of a microwave oven, for example, might include a rotating carousel or multidirectional heating element. The benefit, however, is more even heat distribution to prevent hot and cold spots. Obviously, the benefit will be more attractive to the prospective customer than just the feature. And that essentially is what you're asking the prospective employer to do—i.e., make a purchasing decision. Other features being equal in terms of training and skills, what benefit might you represent over another applicant? Often, these benefits are intangible things, such as attitude and values. Employers frequently rank attitude as a tiebreaker in their hiring decisions. If you have a bad attitude, fix it. If you have a good one, promote it.

The three basic elements of the Minute Pitch are name, abilities (values, skills, interests), and accomplishments. That's pretty simple, but it's a pretty short statement. Employers want to hear action-oriented statements. Think of what benefits or contributions you may have made in your previous jobs, such as meeting deadlines, saving money, making a profit, having an idea, or creating a new product or service. How was the company better off for your involvement? A few suggested action words include *maximized, designed, coordinated, initiated, implemented, maintained, operated, improved, expedited, constructed, eliminated, controlled, created, developed, directed, fixed, increased, completed, changed, achieved, administered,* and *assembled.*

This short personal presentation should be rehearsed with a partner until it sounds natural, credible, sincere, clear, and persuasive, Howard said. That done, you're almost ready for the main event—the actual job interview. This process arms you with the answer to one of the "killer questions" in job interviews: "Tell me about yourself." It's called a "killer" question because its maddening simplicity has caused otherwise sensible people either to go blank and speechless or to babble ad nauseam. But having thought through the process of a personal mission statement, an objective statement, and a Minute Pitch, there's no good reason for your tongue to embarrass you.

Two other killer questions, according to an article in the *National Business Employment Weekly* by Ken Glickman, an executive with Right Associates, a national business outplacement firm, are "Why did you leave your last job?" and "What do you really want to do?"[1] The only one you should fear is why you left your last job. The interviewer's ulterior motive may be just to see how you handle a question that makes most people squirm a bit. Again, resist any temptation to bad-mouth your previous employer. This is a name-rank-and-serial-number question—i.e., you are only obligated to explain if you quit the job. If your employer terminated it, you can give an official reason—downsizing, etc.—and beyond that only the employer can explain the employer's actions.

When it comes to what you really want to do, you now should have this nailed down better than anyone else this interviewer has interviewed. Go for it.

POSTSCRIPT

After some additional testing, Juanita Tompkins urged Jerry to consider going into graphic design. He agreed, and, with the help of federal funding from the American Recovery and Reinvestment Act, he has enrolled in classes at the local community college toward that end.

It looks like Jerry Davenport's couch potato days may be coming to an end.

9

WORK
OUTSIDE THE BOX

Maybe you've done it all. When it comes to your
particular occupation, you've been there, done
that. So has Jeff Pederson.

Pederson, owner of JPED Consulting, LLC
(www.jpedconsulting.com) in Colorado Springs,
Colorado, has done branding, marketing, and
consulting work for more than 150 organizations
over thirty years. He has worked for three publish-
ing companies and consulted with fourteen others.
He has helped engineer a corporate turnaround
situation producing a $4 million net income in
twenty-three months. He has been the chief execu-
tive officer of a company, started five subsidiaries,
owned his own business, reviewed thousands of
résumés, and hired hundreds of people.

But it's not enough.

The successful job-seeker today must be able to break through the clutter in the marketplace with a clear personal brand.

In more recent years, Pederson said, he has had to learn to communicate a brand statement in no more than ten seconds to "break through the clutter" in conversations. Simply, an individual's brand goes one more step beyond the mission and vision statements by adding value—a "deliverable," a promise, a benefit. And now he teaches the process to others.

For example, Pederson's own branding statement: "I'm a marketing and business growth consultant, and I do marketing and branding work for organizations and help them create new ideas and grow their profitability." He explained, "I use buzz words that work for business owners—I capture their attention. I don't say I'm a 'business consultant.' I say I'm a business *growth* consultant—revenues and profitability, where every business owner's ears are going to perk up a little bit."

A great résumé is no longer sufficient. The successful job-seeker today must be able to break through the clutter in the marketplace with a clear personal brand. He must strategically network and even volunteer his services in places where people will see his value and recommend him to someone else he's never met. He must understand the new high-tech tools of social networks—Linkedin, Facebook, Twitter—where many of these relationships and connections are now forged.

Linkedin.com especially is a force to be reckoned with in the business realm, with forty million members and thousands more joining it every week, according to Pederson. People have reported great success using this powerful networking tool, especially by asking their first-generation contacts to introduce them to others in strategic positions within a desirable potential employer organization. But the job seeker still needs to be able to package and sell himself clearly and succinctly with such network contacts.

"The thirty-second elevator speech is too long," said Pederson.

And job prospectors need to cultivate a self-employed attitude even after finding a new job. Self-employment may not be for everybody, but everybody needs to have a self-employed attitude. More than that, for a growing number of people, the answer may be more than adopting a self-employed attitude, but actually becoming self-employed.

JOBS—OR WORK?

For me, the lightbulb went on after the door closed on my second career. The first one—journalism—lasted twenty years, long enough for three different jobs. But by 1987, when I began looking for my fourth newspaper position, something had changed. In the 1970s, I used to get nice, personalized, hand-signed letters from editors telling me there were no openings, but they'd keep my application on file. This time, there were no such letters. In fact, I was disturbed to find that it was the rare exception to get the courtesy of any response, even when I was applying for actual openings advertised in the *Editor & Publisher* trade journal. I tended to assume that this was a recent development peculiar to my profession.

My second career—public relations—lasted only six years. One Monday morning I came in at nine and was literally out on the street by nine thirty. The guy after me was out by ten. Since then, I have been told there's a neologism for that, too—being "streeted." I immediately began looking for a replacement job and began to experience, as Yogi Berra is alleged to have said, "Déjà vu all over again." PR had become another bear market. The few available positions I could find to apply for in my town paid so little that I began to consider something that had been only an attractive pipe dream before—working for myself, being my own boss.

I soon found that there might not be many good *jobs*, but there was a good deal of *work* available if I knew where to look for it. The CEO of a local public relations/advertising agency, for example, acquired several new clients, but said he was leery of staffing up aggressively for the long term. Giving me some assignments as an independent contractor helped both him and me. Then, to my surprise, my former employer offered me the same arrangement on a larger scale, and this company ironically became the biggest client of Adams Business Communications. ABC, in turn, provided me the base from which to strike out in some other directions.

I did some freelance writing for business publications, which has been better for my professional development, visibility, and education than for pure income. (Tip: Self-employment is more lucrative if you charge on the billable-hour rather than flat-fee basis, as writers are more usually paid. Unless you can do an exceptionally fast turnaround, flat fees get eaten up quickly in time-intensive projects like writing and communications.) I also continued to write books, which was personally rewarding but compounded the problem experienced by self-employed people everywhere, especially in start-up situations: long hours. But if the investment stage proves successful in the long run, it will have been worth it.

ABC also served as the launch-pad for a second enterprise, a management consulting service called WorkLife, Inc. This service was aimed at helping managers and employees find fulfillment in the work itself through an improved work environment and corporate culture. My partner, a former labor negotiator named Sam Lombardo, lost his job five months after I lost mine. When we first started discussing the WorkLife concept, which involved a unique, if not radical, methodology, Sam and I were both employed and would never have had the courage—or recklessness—to quit our jobs to start such a venture. He was newly married with a baby on the way, and I was months away from sending my oldest child to college. The timing was what's sometimes called counterintuitive. Translation: A sane person would not have planned it that way.

But unemployment gave us the boost that we needed. The job is dead—long live the new career!

MEET THE "PICS" OF THE WORKFORCE

It was a different world when C. Northcote Parkinson published his delightful little book *Parkinson's Law* in 1958. U.S. and British businesses were fat and happy, and lifetime employment was the norm. Parkinson's first law states: "Work expands to fill the time available for its completion." The book was a good-natured poke at the bureaucratic inefficiencies of that old paradigm, with all of its meetings, committees, recreation leagues, speakers' bureaus, and gold watches, before there was any reason for entire industries to fear for their corporate survival or to worry about a foreign competitor walking away with the marbles.

It's time for a new social contract recognizing current realities in the marketplace.

As we now know all too well, it was that complacent attitude that inadvertently paved the way for those predatory incursions in the first place. Today, that hidebound view would be like wading into an Amazon River tributary and waiting for the piranha to gather. The new reality might be more like a paraphrase of one of the laws of thermodynamics: "Jobs may come and go, but work is neither created nor destroyed. It is only changed in form." I am calling it "Newton's Corollary" in honor of the great English mathematician.

The largest nongovernmental employer in the United States for years has been Manpower, Inc., the agency for temporary workers. Temps or contingency workers comprise an estimated one-quarter of the American workforce. That includes 22 million part-time workers, 9 million contract workers, and 1.2 million temporary employees, according to the U.S. Bureau of Labor Statistics. And these are no longer confined to secretarial, clerical, and other support personnel, but comprise an increasingly diverse workforce, including engineers, legal and medical workers, and other professional services. Some beauty salons are even paying temporary workers to give permanents.

Former corporate executioner Alan Downs says it's time for a new social contract recognizing current realities in the market-place, including an emerging class of workers he calls PICs—professional independent contract employees—or contract professionals. PICs resemble temps, but Downs argues they should command higher fees even than permanent employees because they bear the responsibility for their own benefits (health, life, and retirement), professional development, self-marketing, and downtime between projects.

Downs writes in *Corporate Executions*:

> Changing the corporation from a roster of employees to a loosely connected network of contract professionals will dramatically shrink the size in number of employees and space of today's corporation. With this shrinking will come a shift in responsibility from the shoulders of the corporation to the workers. No longer will the company bear the time-consuming, parental responsibility for providing the material needs of its workers; nor will it be required to police their day-to-day activities. Instead, the company can focus time and attention on essential business strategy.[1]

Indeed, the concept is not all that new. Building contractors, craftsmen, carpenters, and painters, as Downs points out, have been working like this for years. And now consultants and independent contractors like me are doing it as well. What's new is the challenge to our society, not just to accept it as a growing way of life, but to make provision for such work within the mainstream of our economy. To Alan Downs's proposal, I give a hearty amen. I had to give up collecting any state unemployment benefits after a few weeks of trying unsuccessfully to adjust that against the sporadic and unpredictable income I was starting to generate as a freelancer. Losing that safety net certainly accelerated my move to become self-sufficient! In so many ways—from taxes to benefits to government red tape on things like home offices—the life of an independent contractor does not entirely compute yet in America, but it's getting there.

Does self-employment appeal to you? Have you had the urge to start a business? Many new ventures fail. Fortunately, there are more helpful resources now than ever before for budding entrepreneurs. A particularly helpful one is *BusinessWeek*'s Business Exchange entrepreneurship blog at http://bx.businessweek.com/entrepreneurship/blogs/. Among its thousands of articles, searchable by topic, chances are good for finding what you're looking for—whether it's "9 Things Invented or Discovered by Accident" or "America's Weirdest Businesses." Check it out.

HOME, INC.

The fact that headcount-conscious, downsizing U.S. corporations are turning increasingly to outsourcing fulfills the prediction of Newton's Corollary by creating enormous new opportunities for entrepreneurs and the growing class of professional independent contractors that Alan Downs describes. In many ways, the historic trend in the relationship between work and life is coming full circle, to the point of giving entirely new meaning to the term "cottage industry."

Companies large and small are being affected by these changes in corporate culture and personal lifestyle. The Big Four accounting firm of Ernst & Young, for example, adopted "hoteling" for some workers. Instead of being assigned offices and working behind desks, the company's management consultants in some cities spend most of their time out at client sites. When they are in the office, they are assigned working space in some common office areas set aside for the purpose. Elsewhere, information technology equipment, such as laptop computers and cellular routers, make it increasingly possible to perform many jobs from anywhere, including a home or a car.

Efficiency-minded American business is discovering that in many cases the person who works at home is actually more productive than the one in the office. An average 15 to 20 percent increase in productivity has been associated with working at home. Factors include fewer interruptions and distractions than in the traditional workplace with all of its meetings, announcements, paperwork, and water-cooler chitchat. But it would be premature to pronounce the traditional work environment obsolete. Clearly, working at home is only applicable to certain types of enterprise, generally in the area of services—such as computer and other information workers, accountants, sales reps, insurance adjusters, and market research analysts.

The self-employed at home have a more direct incentive: produce or don't eat.

There is also the intangible human factor. Those who have been working at home to date may be those most equipped and motivated to do so, and therefore more likely to succeed. As their ranks grow approximately 20 percent a year, only time will tell if this trend holds up. Telecommuters, for example, have to justify themselves to their bosses and coworkers with hard results to avoid the unspoken suspicion of lounging about. The self-employed at home have a more direct incentive: produce or don't eat. There is no organizational safety net beneath them if they slack off. But, as one who routinely pays those dues, I see nothing wrong with being responsible for myself. Anything else is probably doomed to fail in the long run, anyway.

I will be the first to admit that the home office environment or self-employment is not for everybody. To paraphrase the old saying about the lawyer who represents himself: "The worker who goes into business for himself has a fool for a boss." That is to say, quitting your job to work for yourself is no automatic solution to the troubled career. If some of your woes are of your own making or due to your own shortcomings, hiring yourself to be your new boss may do no more than trade one set of problems for another.

Not everyone is sufficiently self-disciplined or self-directed by nature to work alone, just as some people are not by nature team players. According to management consultant and professor Harry Levinson, there are some psychological needs that the workplace provides that are absent at home—principally a sense of achievement and connectedness, the "need to depend on others and be depended upon."[2] Levinson is founder of the Levinson Institute, Waltham, Massachusetts, which focuses on the psychological aspects of leadership in organizations. These factors are remarkably reminiscent of the first two of our three universal human needs—relationship, impact, and integrity.

Brad Schepp, author of *The Telecommuter's Handbook*, says a sense of isolation and disconnectedness is the biggest drawback for the worker at home. "People who telecommute full-time are especially prone to feeling they are no longer part of the team. Psychologists call this company-connectedness feeling organizational identification, and it is important because how much you identify with your company affects how high you'll climb the corporate ladder."[3] Some of that isolation can be combated with commonsense approaches—staying in touch with others by phone, lunch dates, e-mail, and just getting out of the office periodically.

Then there are others who work fine solo but face the opposite problem—too many intrusions and distractions from friends, associates, and other family members. Or maybe it's the temptation to distract themselves by playing computer solitaire, listening to the radio, watching television, surfing the Internet, or chatting excessively on the phone. Possessing a vivid imagination for failure, an acute drivenness, and the gift of worrying, I have rarely experienced those distractions for long before I start barking, either at others to back off or at myself to get serious. If anything, my own temptation is the opposite—to let my work life intrude into my personal and family life through crash projects and long hours, which is another classic pitfall.

HOW TO "DE-JOB"

If you lack natural discipline, I recommend importing some. Doors are wonderful devices for screening things out. If people can't take a hint, post a biohazard sign or some other toxic symbol on the outside. If you're the dense one, try posting a picture of your former boss on the inside (at least for a while). That's always good for a reality check. If you don't have a picture of your former boss, hang up a picture of Kim Jong-il or Godzilla and pretend. This is also where goals come in. Set deadlines for yourself, just as you would have if you worked downtown, and withhold incentives—food or work breaks—until you have reached them. But once you have met your goals and deadlines, take time to reward yourself. Now you deserve it.

If you are too driven and your family and friends have forgotten your name, schedule some downtime. If you're too busy to do that, you're too busy. Go back to square one and revisit your personal mission—why you were put here on earth. It probably wasn't to spend more time in the office.

Yes, there are downsides to the post-job lifestyle—or "dejobbing," as William Bridges calls it—but the advantages are just as real. Ri Regina, a former technology manager, said that even though she's an extrovert, the home office lifestyle suits her as long as she can manage to get outside several times a week.

"I love coming down here and sitting in my office," she said, "and I have got my dog sitting at my feet, I have my bayberry candle burning on my desk, I have my CD player with my collection of CDs from home and the library. I have wonderful music playing all day, the windows open, looking at the soft snow falling."

Roy Peterson, a former health insurance manager, is particularly fond of not having to wear a tie and fight rush hour traffic.

"There are a number of upsides," he said. "There is a lot less wear and tear on you and your car and your clothes and everything else because you don't have to go anywhere. There are two hours a day you save because you are not in a car just trying to get to the place that you are going to work. That's a lot of time—ten hours a week. So, basically one advantage is you get a day a week back. And you don't have to wear a tie.

"There is a lot more flexibility. If my daughter has a track meet at four o'clock, I can probably work things out so I can be there, and no one is going to howl about it and I'll still get as much or more done as I would have otherwise. With the technological means available to us, you just don't have to go as many places as you used to. It is more comfortable, and it feels good. I get up in the morning and go to work by going down a flight of stairs."

YOU & CO

It is helpful to think of these different work environments as a continuum. At one end is the traditional workplace with an executive suite, security guards, coffee stations, high-end machinery or office equipment, and suits and ties or hard hats and ear protection. At the other extreme is the sun-porch office where a pensive writer in jeans and an absurd orange-and-white cat named Roscoe share an eight-foot-square space with a desk, personal computer, printer, phone, stacks of books, a bottle of antacid tablets, several cacti, and a sprawling spider plant.

In between are the various shades of gray, such as the telecommuters and hotelers, who are still employed by an organization but work mostly outside. Then there's job-sharing, where two part-timers might divide the responsibilities of a full-time position, though probably without the benefits. Some people only want to work for an employer part-time because they are engaged in what's called a composite career. These are the people who work different jobs or combine employment with some entrepreneurial enterprise, like the art dealer who works in a machine shop by day.

This is the place on the continuum where self-employment begins, with multiple bosses called clients and customers. William Bridges urges post-job workers to organize "You & Co." and run it as a business.[4] Almost paradoxically, it combines specialization (defining a narrow market niche for yourself) and diversification (with multiple activities, customers, and income streams). I don't have to look far for an example. My own Adams Business Communications was a diverse umbrella for several activities, including public relations as a subcontractor, freelance business writing, and authoring books and novels.

Increasingly, the line is blurring between traditional businesses and one-man bands like ABC. With state-of-the-art information technology, these virtual offices in dens and sun porches are capable of providing services that once would have required leased space and maybe several support personnel. When two or more of these mini-organizations join forces for the purpose of a particular project, it is sometimes called an adhocracy, a strategic alliance, or a virtual corporation.

> **Increasingly, the line is blurring between traditional businesses and one-man bands.**

That's the shape of things to come. Even stranger is the emergence of virtual products—custom-produced goods that do not even exist until customers order them. And increasingly, customers will be ordering them not from a store or snail-mail order, but through the vehicle of electronic commerce through a service such as Amazon. Early last century, the Model T was available in any color, Henry Ford said, as long as it was black. Now, many believe that customization—tailoring individual products and services to personal specifications—is the star to follow.

The economy of the future also entails radical changes in the workforce itself, as well as other trends that may turn out positive for some workers. According to the Mass Career Customization, "In the next five years, there will be a 6 million-person gap between the supply and demand of knowledge workers."[5] That's good news for knowledge workers—a term coined by management expert Peter Drucker in reference to medical professionals, teachers, engineers, scientists, and growing ranks of people in the field of information technology.

Combined with other trends—a majority female workforce, the digital technology revolution, continuing changes in the traditional family structure—this projected shortage of skilled labor is giving rise to another trend, called "mass career customization." This essentially means more flexible working arrangements such as compressed workweeks, predictable schedules, "telework," and telecommuting. While not brand-new trends, they can be expected to take hold as never before.

Total work hours for dual-earner couples are increasing, for example. In 1970, couples worked a combined average of 52.5 hours per week. Couples now work a combined average of 63.1 hours per week, and almost 70 percent of them work more than 80 hours per week. Employees are increasingly likely to be both working and providing care to a friend or family member. Currently, 59 percent of those caring for a relative or friend work and manage care-giving responsibilities at the same time.

Expanding longevity, ongoing interest, and financial need are prompting more mature workers to stay in the work force. By 2015, older workers will constitute 20 percent—one out of every five workers—of the total work force. Approximately 31 million workers—about 23 percent of the workforce—are low-wage. Roughly 40 percent of low-wage workers work non-standard hours.[6] Many of these individuals want more workplace flexibility. Many will seek those conditions through self-employment and home-based enterprises. According to one report, employees saved more than $1,700 per year in gasoline and wear and tear on their vehicles by working at home an average of 2.5 days a week while also saving energy.[7]

According to Dent, here are some more traditional job categories that lend themselves to home-based business and independent contractors:

- Accounting and bookkeeping
- Advertising and promotion
- Art and promotion materials
- Career counseling and outplacement
- Editorials and writing
- Field sales
- Janitorial and maintenance
- Market research and analysis
- MIS and computer software and systems
- Personality testing and evaluations
- Phone sales and telemarketing
- Secretarial and office production services
- Tax and tax planning
- Training and educational materials.[8]

Work-at-home.org offers a thought-provoking list of hundreds of home-based business ideas—from Abstracting Service to Yard Sign Distributorship—at http://www.work-at-home.org.

THE ULTIMATE
MISSION

GOING *FORWARD* UNTO ETERNITY
AS WE GO *BACK* TO WORK

A few years ago Jeff Taylor took probably the biggest gamble of his professional life: He shelled out $4 million for one thirty-second ad—at the 1999 Super Bowl. It was a truly memorable commercial called "When I Grow Up . . ." You've probably seen it. Young children speak directly to the camera, saying:

"When I grow up, I want to file all day."

"I want to claw my way up to middle management."

"Be replaced on a whim."

"I want to have a brown nose."

"I want to be a yes-man. . . ."

". . . . yes-woman."

"Yes, sir. Coming, sir."

"Anything for a raise, sir."

"When I grow up . . . ."

"I want to be underappreciated."

"Be paid less for doing the same job."

"I want to be forced into early retirement."

Then across the screen appear the words "What did you want to be?" It was a golden moment in advertising—as well as in the quest for meaning and purpose in the lives of millions. Who could help being moved at the sound of such cynical statements from the mouths of babes? And then how many of us took it to the next step and recognized our own stifled and broken dreams? One thing for sure: The message touched a nerve in many and made an indelible impression for Taylor's up-and-coming Monster.com online job search service.

Not doing what we were really born to do is a one-person-at-a-time tragedy.

As Taylor recalls, "Amid all those ads for cars and beer, it was an outrageously optimistic statement with an ironic twist about how our childhood dreams get compromised. The ad worked because it captured the voice and personality of Monster. We aired that commercial 4,000 times in 1999, and it put us on the map."[1]

The optimism Taylor alludes to is the possibility that as long as we're still breathing, dreams can come true. Frustrations in life may be inevitable, but they don't have to be permanent. Not doing what we were really born to do is a one-person-at-a-time tragedy. If this is true for television audiences of $4 million commercials, how much truer is it for believers? King David understood this: "Delight yourself in the Lord and he will give you the desires of your heart" (Psalm 37:4).

So, how about it? What did you want to be when you grew up? Really.

THE CALLER BEHIND THE CALLING

The average time between job situations, according to some surveys, is nine months—long enough to create new life. Make it a time to find a new life. Employment experts say there are at least two essentials for making a good case to the future employer, and they also may apply to self-employment. Unfortunately, they are two qualities that the beaten-down victim of the downsizing wave is least likely to possess in abundance—ability to demonstrate competence and an enthusiastic demeanor.

Enthusiasm is a magical word. It comes from the Greek and literally means "to be filled with God" *(theos/theus)*. It may seem a cruel irony that when an individual is most beaten down, he or she must somehow appear the most upbeat and confident to hope to win the favor of another employer. Truly, this would seem to require the intervention of the divine and miraculous.

Some experts suggest getting motivated with clearer values and even spiritual insights by writing your own obituary. List your key accomplishments, what people will remember you for, and the additional things you might yet achieve. "People are always amazed at how few good years they have left," writes David Noer in *Healing the Wounds*.[2] The point is not to become further discouraged, but to appreciate the value of the remaining time and to make the most of it.

This brings us back full circle to our personal mission in life. How do we know when we have found it? Richard Nelson Bolles, author of the famous *What Color Is Your Parachute?* a book that is updated annually, is also an Episcopal priest. In the appendix of his books, he states categorically that this search inevitably leads to God—the Caller behind the calling, the Destination at the end of the destiny. The word *mission* itself—from the Latin *mittere*, meaning "to send," as in transmit or remit—implies a Sender. Similarly, *vocation* derives from the Latin "to call," as in "evoke" (to call out) or "revoke" (to call back).

"If you would figure out your Mission in life, you must also be willing to think about God in connection with your job-hunt," Bolles wrote. In fact, Bolles believes each person has three missions: discovering God, making this world a better place, and exercising "your greatest gift, which you most delight to use," in your God-given mission.[3] He says that is the talent that "gives us the greatest pleasure from its exercise (it is usually the one which, when we use it, causes us to lose all sense of time)."[4]

When I was newly unemployed, I benefited from small daily doses of work/life wisdom from motivational speaker Jim Rohn via a friend's loaner videotape. Rohn's words rang a bell when he likened our role to the planting of an acorn and God's role to growing the oak tree. He reminded his audience of Christ's words about God's care and concern for the birds of the air and the lilies of the field while men "of little faith" worry about what they will eat, drink, and wear. Rohn said this is God's promise that He will grow the tree if we will plant the seed—i.e., exercise our gifts.

Then it hit me as forcefully as if God had spoken to me personally, though inaudibly: "If you want to know God's will for your life, look at your gifts. He doesn't play games; like the acorn, you already have the ability to perform whatever is in God's plan for you." I began to have a greater assurance that I had something better under me than an earthly safety net—what Scripture calls the "everlasting arms."

Human resources consultant Ralph T. Mattson wrote in *Redeemed Ambition*: "Very important signposts in the matter of selecting careers are the gifts He has willed into your personalities. God's definition of a person is the act of creating him. . . . All the information with which we need to begin the process of career selection already resides within us. We must tap it."[5]

The problem is not that we don't believe in God. Opinion polls indicate that overwhelming numbers of Americans have such a belief; similar numbers of people even pray. The problem is in our "little faith." In some ways, Bolles and others suggest, the problem may even be worse for believers. We ask, "How could

God let this happen to me if He truly loved me?" I know I felt that way after the death of my son. It's called a sense of abandonment.

In a sometimes disturbing and always challenging book, *Bold Love*, Dan Allender argues that our attitude toward God at these times is most akin to actual hatred. We take for granted our unfettered right to exercise free will, but then tacitly accuse God of abandoning us by not intervening when misfortune befalls us. If bitterness and grudges on the human plane sap our strength and rot our bones, what about the spiritual dimension? Neil Anderson says flatly that in his counseling unforgiveness is the number one avenue for occult oppression—in believers. Allender says when faced with injustice and suffering in the world, we have a basic choice in our response between hatred versus gratitude. We can respond to life's circumstances with "humble, quiet grace" or "angry, demanding assertion."[6]

We can respond to life's circumstances with "humble, quiet grace" or "angry, demanding assertion."

God the great Sustainer does not cause our hard times, nor does He generally rescue us out of them. But He does give us the grace, courage, and strength to endure hard times. Many times, that's the factory that produces those character qualities. "The 94% of us who believe in God," Bolles wrote, "usually need a larger conception of God, as we face each new crisis in our life. If you've got an old faith hanging in the closet of your mind, now would be a good time to take it out and dust it off."[7]

Easy for him to say? Not really. Richard Bolles is the brother of Don Bolles, an investigative reporter in Arizona who was killed by a car bomb in 1976 while investigating organized crime and political connections. As a newspaper reporter then myself, I remember Don Bolles's agonizing eleven-day demise. It was the inspiration for the founding of an organization called IRE—

Investigative Reporters and Editors—which I joined. May I suggest that Richard Bolles is intimately acquainted with injustice and suffering. He, too, has faced the choice between humble, quiet grace and angry, demanding assertion and has chosen wisely. That wise choice has resulted in an enormous overflow into the lives of others such as myself.

What is the application? Forgive: forgive the one who fired you. It may be a blessing in disguise in the form of a new future. Forgive yourself. Now is the time you need to stand your tallest—acquiring a nobler character full of grace, courage, and strength. Get right with God. Think of the things for which you have been forgiven. He is the lighthouse. Change your heading.

Instrumental in helping to update this book for the 2000s was laid-off researcher Steve Kipp, quoted earlier. Much of his advice for approaching the issues of career crisis needs no embellishment and bears repeating here.

MY TAKE: STEVE KIPP

This is a marvelous time to become a people-investment person—and to really mean it. Don't get lost in the temptation *only* to network because of the eventual "boomerang" effect upon yourself in landing a future job. We need to ask ourselves as we network, What's the difference between Christian job-searchers networking and the rest of the world? Do we take it seriously that it's better to give than receive? As we search for jobs, are we mindful of others' qualifications and specific job types and do we forward them leads we have? Do we practice Galatians 6:10—"Do good to all people, especially to those who belong to the family of believers"—both as networkers and as people in positions to hire?

Use a multifaceted job search approach. Don't rely upon single methods, and curb over-reliance on want ads, online posted notices, job boards, and job fairs. Develop an all-out "new media" approach—business cards to hand out at networking events and job fairs; a brochure about yourself; offer your net-working "teammates" web link opportunities, etc., to show you are a team player; a website blog page or promotional page about who you are, your accomplishments, your vision, and so on.

Beware the self-help gurus. Some of their message is based upon visualization techniques, "awakening your dream" as if you were a New Age realization adherent. These gurus focus on reinventing yourself using human potential movement, self-ist and/or New Age principles. Unfortunately, these over-whelm the Borders and Amazon and Barnes & Noble shelves. Too many hungry job-seekers, in trying to "reinvent" themselves or recover a lost identity or damaged self-esteem, embrace these self-help gurus' suggestions uncritically.

These advisers too often teach unrealistic positive thinking, failing to take into account economic realities. In the process they promote self-actualization and "it's all about me"—the same kind of thinking that motivates thousands of wannabe American Idols to audition with no real chance of success. And they encourage excessive self-absorption. Yes, unemployed job-seekers need to take serious inventory of their strengths and weaknesses. But who does the vocational "calling"? You? Or God? Often, our "ministry" has more to do with our coworkers than the actual job we're doing. We need to continue to hear God's voice through prayer, people, circumstances, divine appointments, etc.

Authors Dan Miller, John Maxwell, Bob Buford, and others all have some excellent things to say about using this opportunity to focus on significance (impact upon others), meaning, satisfaction, and fulfillment. This comes out best through serving others and being preserving salt and expressive light in the world, moving away from always attempting to attach a legalistic paycheck compensation to all of our service.

Even when we land a job, don't forget the people we met while networking.

Even when we land a job, don't forget the people we met while networking, especially those outside of Christ. They need encouraging, gospel-focused, Word-based follow-up—and just plain friendship, especially those still looking. Through this process, we've not only found a job, but a new "ministry" among fellow networkers. Volunteer at an unemployment support group to pass on all the job-hunt knowledge and resources and referrals you've just acquired. Be a good steward of the pain you endured, because 2 Corinthians 1 says the comfort we received during our time of unemployment wasn't meant exclusively for us, anyway; it was meant for us to promptly pass on to others. Also, help other strugglers financially after you've regained your job balance.

We often have to first die to our self-made dreams and embrace His new vision for where He is taking us. Too many of us prefer to remain in holy huddles where fellow Christians have nurtured us. It's time to become "sent-ones"—the literal meaning of *apostles*. He is sending us into new frontiers of unreached people groups—what used to be called "pagan gentiles." Those folks are now our coworkers and potential coworkers, unique worthy people whom our Lord loves dearly.

NO EARTHLY SECURITY

Life is full of surprises. Like going to work one day and being told your services are no longer required. Most of us prefer a little more predictability in our affairs. We even come to demand that events follow a prescribed course, and when things stray from the script, we become angry and frustrated. As British writer Samuel Butler was quoted as saying in the nineteenth century: "Life is like giving a concert on the violin while learning to play the instrument." Much more recently, American author Saul Bellow likened it to "concertizing and practicing scales at the same time."

Our feelings may get the better of us, Neil Anderson says, but we are responsible for our thinking and our beliefs. "You are not shaped as much by your environment as you are by your perception of your environment," he wrote in *Victory over the Darkness*. "If what you believe does not reflect truth, then what you feel does not reflect reality. . . . Remember: Your emotions are a product of how you perceived the event, not the event itself."[8]

What if you chose to perceive your joblessness as an opportunity for character building? Child psychologists talk about maturity in terms of "frustration tolerance" in everyday life. When I measure myself by that gauge, I shudder. Ornithologists tell of the value of struggle in the birth of a bird. If the egg is punctured to "help" along the process, the hatchling is less likely to survive, failing to develop the requisite strength through the struggle of the birth process. The suggestion is not just that adversity and struggle are a normal part of life, but that they may be essential to life. I recognize that this is not a popular view today, but I believe it's an important perspective for those wounded in the economic theater.

Speaker and author Tim Hansel described this perspective well in his book *You Gotta Keep Dancin'*:

> The big dream in our society is that if we work hard enough, we will eventually be able to experience a life without limitations or difficulties. It is also one of the biggest sources of friction in our society, creating disappointment, unnecessary suffering, and missed opportunities to live a full life. Some people spend their entire life waiting for that which will never, and can never, happen. . . . One of the greatest tragedies of our modern civilization is that you and I can live a trivial life and get away with it. One of the great advantages of pain and suffering is that it forces us to break through our superficial crusts to discover life on a deeper and more meaningful level. . . . Another advantage of disadvantages is that we have the opportunity to be transformed by our suffering.[9]

Here is a question worth pondering: When it comes right down to it, is there any such thing as true earthly security? I think not. And I believe the reason is to turn our hearts toward eternal things. To quote the world's greatest Teacher:

> Do not store up for yourselves treasures on earth, where moth and rust destroy, and where thieves break in and steal. But store up for yourselves treasures in heaven, where moth and rust do not destroy, and where thieves do not break in and steal. For where your treasure is, there your heart will be also. (Matthew 6:19–21)

What are treasures in heaven? In work/life terms, I would suggest they include Bolles's triad of finding God, making the world a better place, and exercising your gift in your life mission. I would also suggest they specifically do not include the accumulation of personal possessions and investing oneself in the climbing of career ladders, especially to the exclusion of family and other human relationships.

Bolles has written eloquently about depression and its emotional and spiritual sources—stored-up anger and a sense of abandonment. There's also a mental source, he says—meaninglessness. In *The Three Boxes of Life*, he tells of a study of surgical patients who found meaning to be the single biggest factor in successful post-operative recovery.

> The more the patient believed that there was no such thing as a meaningless experience, the faster the patient healed. Thus, spiritual survival seems to require that there be some meaning to everything that happens, even if that meaning is not evident to us at the time that we are going through the experience.[10]

I am suggesting that in our adversity this meaning is best found in the context of our personal, earthly mission and in our ultimate, eternal mission. In *Redeemed Ambition*, Ralph Mattson wrote: "If you want to know my will, you will have to come into personal contact with me. If you want to know God's will, you will have to come into personal contact with Him."[11] This may be that opportunity. Don't let it pass you by.

And when those feelings of worthlessness come, remember that the King of Glory was sold for the price of a slave. In the words of James Smith:

> The man is always prosperous who succeeds in doing the will of God. Sold for thirty pieces of silver, yet the pleasure of the Lord prospered in His hand. It does not matter what low value the world may set upon the servant of God, he will be a prosperous man in God's sight if he pleases him.[12]

Remember, too, what the Lord Jesus said on the night He was betrayed: "I have finished the work thou gavest me to do" (John 17:4 KJV). Smith asks the question for all of us: "If He should ask you on that day, 'What was your occupation?' As a Christian what would you answer?"[13] That is, have we done the work He has given us to do? Do we even know what that is? If not, what are we doing about it? Have we been occupied with those things or *pre*-occupied with the things of this world? What is our occupation?

Have we done the work He has given us to do? Do we even know what that is?

Scripture repeatedly exhorts us to live unto eternity. That would seem to call for some reverse engineering, setting our sights on the end in order to plot our steps in the present. Can we not ask the Lord to give us the vision we need to see the way? Can we *go forward* unto eternity as we *go back* to work?

What will be our life-work legacy? Will we be able to say, as the Lord Jesus said, "I have finished the work you have given me to do"?

AFTERWORD

King David said it best: "I was young and now I am old, yet I have never seen the righteous forsaken or their children begging bread" (Psalm 37:25). For believers, that's huge. Note that Scripture doesn't say it can never happen, but it certainly shouldn't be the norm. If you ask yourself what that should look like in the twenty-first century, it will probably lead you to the doorstep of the church. Remember how America caught a brief glimpse of something like religious revival in the days immediately following September 11, 2001? Perhaps God allows America to go through these things partly as a way to bring the church to its feet, truly to become that salt and light it's supposed to be in this crooked and perverse generation.

Or, in this case, maybe it's salt and light and mashed potatoes and gravy. The church of Christ did some wonderful things in and around Ground Zero in New York City in those days after 9/11, and it wasn't just passing out tracts. It was food and other emergency assistance. It was grief counseling. It was helping people make sense of naked terror. It was shoulders to cry on. I know because I was there, and I saw it. It was powerful. But then time passed, and the sands shifted slowly back to complacency.

So, where is the church today? Perhaps this is a major opportunity for Christians to step up to the plate and be that good neighbor to the victims of economic crisis and joblessness. How about using our facilities and our people power to the service of our hurting neighbors? Heed the old marketing maxim: "Find a need and meet it." Thousands of Americans are losing their homes to foreclosure. Can we meet some of that need with temporary shelter? Can we help fill a few bellies, too? And can we minister to their hungry spirits? Why not start seeker-sensitive small group studies of something like Rick Warren's *Purpose Driven Life*—or even this book, *Back to Work!* One thing is for sure: There is unprecedented opportunity here for the church to show itself, as Henry Blackaby calls it, as "God's redemptive agent in the world."

Think about it.

Would you like to continue this discussion?

There's a way:

Go to **www.back2workbook.com**, where there will be an ongoing conversation on the issues discussed in this book as well as a wealth of additional resources to peruse.

APPENDIX:
FOR THE SELF-EMPLOYED

Suppose you don't get another job, but you pursue self-employment. How do you price your services? Here's one formula for calculating a billable hourly rate, which I have adapted from several sources:

Work backward. Say an in-house staffer would be paid $45,000 a year for the same work in your locale. That's the market rate. Divide by 1,500, which is the number of billable hours you might reasonably expect in a year (thirty hours a week times fifty weeks), considering client development, marketing, and other nonbillable time, yielding a base of $30 an hour. In all cases, adapt this to your personal situation. If, for example, you really are billing out forty hours a week, your annual hourly factor would be 2,000 (forty hours a week times fifty weeks).

Then add another 33 percent to cover the cost of taxes and fringe benefits that you bear (for example, Social Security, health insurance, and retirement) plus another factor for your own costs of doing business (overhead, such as rent, equipment, supplies). Some accountants use a 35 percent factor for fringe costs. The overhead cost factor will vary much more, depending on the nature of your business. If you're a writer, like me, you may not have much more than the costs of a personal computer, paper, long-distance phone calls, and the like. Check with an accountant for guidance.

In our hypothetical case, those three calculations would look like this:

$30 (base rate) + $10 (33 percent fringes)
+ $6 (20 percent overhead) = $46 per hour.

Therefore, you know you would be charging a fair rate somewhere around $45 to $50 an hour. With a little research you also may be able to obtain suggested flat fee schedules from professional organizations and publications. That gives you the flexibility to bid a job two different ways. If you're really hungry, the flat fee is more likely to win the job because your prospective client knows his expense is capped. The downside for you is that things generally take longer than projected, and you may end up eating those costs.

ACKNOWLEDGMENTS

I am greatly indebted to the following people for all of their kindness and assistance, without which *Back to Work!* would never have been possible: My friends Steve Kipp, Brian Clements, Mark Carlen, Jim Pfaff. And special thanks to my friends at Moody who had such vision and enthusiasm for this book, especially Randall Payleitner and Greg Thornton.

NOTES

Chapter 1: The Job Squeeze

1. "The Downsizing of America," *New York Times*, series, March 3 to March 9, 1996.

2. Richard Pérez-Peña, "Times Co. Announces Temporary Salary Cuts," *New York Times*, March 26, 2009, http://www.nytimes.com/2009/03/27/business/media/27times.html.

3. "February Newspaper Layoffs Total 1,492 People," *News Cycle*, March 3, 2009, http://news-cycle.blogspot.com/2009/03/february-newspaper-layoffs-total-2073.html.

4. "The Math Behind the Likely Jobless Recovery," Associated Press, msnbc.com, August 10, 2009.

5. Mortimer Zuckerman, "The Economy Is Even Worse Than You Think," *The Wall Street Journal*, July 14, 2009, http://online.wsj.com/article/SB124753066246235811.html.

6. Ibid.

7. Catherine Rampell, "As Layoffs Surge, Women May Pass Men in Job Force," February 5, 2009, http://www.nytimes.com/2009/02/06/business/06women.html.

8. Fisch, McLeod, Brenman, "Did You Know?" http://www.youtube.com/watch?v=EOpA9kNb3fk.

9. William Bridges, *JobShift: How to Prosper in a World without Jobs* (Reading, Mass.: Addison-Wesley, 1994), viii.

10. Ibid.

11. Harry S. Dent Jr., *JobShock: Four New Principles Transforming Our Work and Business* (New York: St. Martin's, 1995), 7.

12. John Naisbitt and Patricia Aburdene, *Re-inventing the Corporation: Transforming Your Job and Your Company for the New Information Society* (New York: Warner, 1985), 14.

13. Steve Vogel, "Age Discrimination Claims Jump, Worrying EEOC, Worker Advocates," *Washington Post*, July 16, 2009, http://www.washingtonpost.com/wp-dyn/content/article/2009/07/15/AR2009071503760.html?hpid=sec-nation.

14. Dennis Cauchon, "Older males hurt more by this recession," *USA Today*, July 29, 2009, http://www.usatoday.com/money/economy/employment/2009-07-29-oldermales_N.htm

15. Cliff Hakim, *We Are All Self-Employed: Achieving Independence, Collaboration, and Fulfillment Inside or Outside Organizations* (San Francisco:

Berrett-Koehler, 1994), 13. David M. Noer, in *Healing the Wounds: Overcoming the Trauma of Layoffs and Revitalizing Downsized Organizations* (San Francisco: Jossey-Bass, 1993), 143, makes a similar point, as does Alan Downs in *Corporate Executions*, 206–07. Downs's work on this subject is discussed in chapter 9 of this book, "Work Outside the Box."

16. Noer, *Healing the Wounds*, 139.

17. Judith M. Bardwick, *Danger in the Comfort Zone: From Boardroom to Mailroom: How to Break the Entitlement Habit That's Killing American Business* (New York: Amacom, 1991), 18–19.

18. Ibid., 28.

19. Noer, *Healing the Wounds*, xv.

20. Ibid., 151.

Chapter 4: The Wave of Change

1. "The Downsizing of America," *New York Times*, series, March 3 to March 9, 1996.

2. Anne Wilson Schaef and Diane Fassel, *The Addictive Organization: Why We Overwork, Cover Up, Pick Up the Pieces, Please the Boss, and Perpetuate Sick Organizations* (New York: Harper & Row, 1988), 132.

3. David M. Noer, *Healing the Wounds: Overcoming the Trauma of Layoffs and Revitalizing Downsized Organizations* (San Francisco: Jossey-Bass, 1993), 136, 141.

4. Ibid., 13.

5. Ibid., 52.

6. J. Leonard Kaye and Julie Rubenstein, eds., *The Wisdom of Baltasar Gracián: A Practical Manual for Good and Perilous Times* (New York: Pocket, 1992), 17.

7. Thomas Gordon, *Leadership Effectiveness Training* (New York: Wyden, 1977), 75.

8. Cliff Hakim, *When You Lose Your Job: Laid Off, Fired, Early Retired, Relocated, Demoted, Unchallenged* (San Francisco: Berrett-Koehler, 1993), 36, 187.

9. Noer, *Healing the Wounds*, 143.

Chapter 5: At the Core

1. David M. Noer, *Healing the Wounds: Overcoming the Trauma of Layoffs and Revitalizing Downsized Organizations* (San Francisco: Jossey-Bass, 1993), 151.

2. Lawrence J. Crabb Jr., *Understanding People: Deep Longings for Relationship* (Grand Rapids: Zondervan, 1987), 114.

3. Ibid., 113.

4. Perry Pascarella, and Mark A. Frohman, *The Purpose-Driven Organization: Unleashing the Power of Direction and Commitment* (San Francisco: Jossey-Bass, 1989), 35.

5. James C. Collins, and Jerry I. Porras, *Built to Last: Successful Habits of Visionary Companies* (New York: HarperBusiness, 1994), 73.

6. Ibid., 70–71.

Chapter 6: The Journey of Self-Discovery

1. Cliff Hakim, *When You Lose Your Job: Laid Off, Fired, Early Retired, Relocated, Demoted, Unchallenged* (San Francisco: Berrett-Koehler, 1993), 182.

2. "Preparing the Workers of Today for the Jobs of Tomorrow," July 2009, http://www.whitehouse.gov/administration/eop/cea/Jobs-of-the-Future/.

3. *Occupational Outlook Handbook*, http://www.bls.gov/oco.

4. William Bridges, *JobShift: How to Prosper in a World without Jobs* (Reading, Mass.: Addison-Wesley, 1994), 77.

5. Ibid., 79–82.

6. George Barna, *Leaders on Leadership: Wisdom, Advice, and Encouragement on the Art of Leading God's People* (Regal Books, 1998).

7. Buzzell, Boa, and Perkins, *The Leadership Bible* (Zondervan, 1998).

Chapter 7: Overcoming Rejection

1. Stanley Milgram, et al., *The Individual in a Social World: Essays and Experiments* (New York: McGraw-Hill, 1992), 259–75.

Chapter 8: Survival and Self-Marketing

1. Ken Glickman, "Learn to Handle 'Killer' Interview Questions," *National Business Employment Weekly*, 4 February 1996.

Chapter 9: Work Outside the Box

1. Alan Downs, *Corporate Executions* (New York: Amacom, 1995), 206–7.

2. Harry Levinson, quoted in Todd Shryock, "Telecommuting Has Value, but Don't Jump in Too Quickly," *Small Business News*, Cleveland, February 1996, 68–69.

3. Brad Schepp, *The Telecommuter's Handbook: How to Work for a Salary—without Ever Leaving the House* (New York: Pharos, 1990), 23.

4. William Bridges, *JobShift: How to Prosper in a World without Jobs* (Reading, Mass.: Addison-Wesley, 1994), 109–12.

5. http://www.masscareercustomization.com/about_mcc.html.

6. National Advisory Commission on Workplace Flexibility, "Public Policy Platform on Flexible Work Arrangements," *Georgetown Law*, 12.

7. Ibid, 28.

8. Harry S. Dent, Jr., *JobShock: Four New Principles Transforming Our Work and Business* (New York: St. Martin's, 1995), 283.

Chapter 10: The Ultimate Mission: Going *Forward* Unto Eternity as We Go *Back* to Work

1. Jeff Taylor and Doug Hardy, *Monster Careers: How to Land the Job of Your Life* (New York: Penguin Group, 2004), 27.

2. David M. Noer, *Healing the Wounds: Overcoming the Trauma of Layoffs and Revitalizing Downsized Organizations* (San Francisco: Jossey-Bass, 1993), 153.

3. Richard Nelson Bolles, *The 1996 What Color Is Your Parachute?* (Berkeley, Calif.: Ten Speed Press, 1996), 449.

4. Ibid., 458.

5. Ralph T. Mattson, *Redeemed Ambition: Balancing the Drive to Succeed in Your Work* (Chicago: Moody, 1995), 110.

6. Dan B. Allender, and Tremper Longman III, *Bold Love: The Courageous Practice of Life's Ultimate Influence* (Colorado Springs, Colo.: NavPress, 1992), 63.

7. Bolles, *What Color Is Your Parachute?* 95.

8. Neil T. Anderson, *Victory over the Darkness: Realizing the Power of Your Identity in Christ* (Ventura, Calif.: Regal, 1990), 179–80, 199.

9. Tim Hansel, *You Gotta Keep Dancin'* (Elgin, Ill.: David C. Cook, 1985), 94–96.

10. Richard Nelson Bolles, *The Three Boxes of Life: And How to Get Out of Them* (Berkeley, Calif.: Ten Speed Press, 1978, 1981), 354.

11. Mattson, *Redeemed Ambition*, 109.

12. James Smith, *Handfuls of Purpose for Christian Workers and Bible Students: Series I–III* (Grand Rapids: William B. Eerdmans Publishing Co., 1971, originally published 1947), 100.

13. Ibid., 109.